FREESTYLE

PROMOTIONS
and The 7 Simple Steps to Getting Started

Latif Mercado

Other books by
Latif Mercado

Freestyle For Life
Feastyle
Yes Yes Y'all
Books 1, 2, and 3

Mentor advice has been printed by permission from the following promoters; Charlie Rodriguez, Luis Pinto, Hassan Martinez, James Rios, Chuck Lamagra, Nick Huminski, JI Starr.

Published by
La' Entertainment
Monroe, NC 28110
Tel: 704-226-8900

Freestyle Promotions
ISBN: 978-0-9993189-0-4
Copyright © 2017 by La' Entertainment

Manufactured in the United States of America

DEDICATED TO

This book is dedicated to Freestyle promoters everywhere. You have played an integral part in our industry. Your love and respect for the genre has helped maintain it for many years. You took the risk many refused, and through thick and thin you persisted. Because of you, many of us have continued to make a living doing what we love most. I pray that you find this book, not as a threat, but rather in honor of you, and all you have done.

Thank you

Latif Mercado

SPECIAL THANKS

Though many working hours I spend all by myself, I
in no way work alone! My job wouldn't even exist if it
wasn't because of the many people who are behind
what I do. Artists, Promoters, Managers, Club
Owners, Sub Agents, Talent Buyers, Sponsors, and of
course the fans are all a huge part of my career, and
my life. Of course if I would write everyone's name
who played a role, I would have to dedicate an entire
book solely to them, so I won't do that. Instead I will
give a vague reference to those who play an vital role
in my career. And with that said, I begin: To all the
artists who have given me the opportunity to be
involved in their careers, giving me the privilege of
placing them on my roster, an important tool for my
business. Whether exclusive or not, I am blessed and
totally appreciative for the respect you give me as a
professional. To the producers who have created this
music. Had it not been for you, none of this would've
been possible. For you I stand and remove my hat in
reverence of all you've done. To the struggling
producer, still trying to *make* his mark, and the hit
makers whose mark has already been imprinted into

the hearts of millions of fans around the world. I will always be grateful to you, and have the utmost respect for all you've done. To all the DJs, whose passion has kept our music spinning throughout the years. Yes I know, it's a difficult genre, but you did it anyway. Thank you! To my promoters, many I call friend. We've seen each other's family grow, and our long conversations outside of business has placed our relationship in a whole other place. To the fans, both in general, and those who over the years have also become my friends. I've been blessed with something so special, and that is the opportunity to have made friends all over the country and abroad, something that would never have been possible had it not been for this business. And of course to this incredible genre we call Freestyle Music. You've given me a great life. Made raising my family easy and enjoyable. You placed some very special people in my path, and most of all, you've introduced me to my wife. I am forever indebted to you, and therefore vow to protect you, help nurture you, and do all I can to make sure that future generations are aware of you and the contribution you've given to the world of music.

MEET THE MENTORS

It took a whole lot for me to even get up the nerve to ask these Legendary Freestyle Club Promoters if they would be willing to share some of their tips, tricks and techniques with those interested in possibly pursuing a similar career in Freestyle club promotions. I mean, what was I thinking? These people had worked most of their adult lives as promoters, struggling to raise the money, negotiate the talent, secure the venue, and then spend day after day practically begging people to attend their event, and I have the nerve to ask them to just give away their hard knock experience to a bunch of strangers?

With bank accounts on empty, and VIPs no longer picking up their phones, these determined individuals would push ahead as if they could somehow predict the success that would lie just around the corner. The pleas from loved ones totally annihilated by their unrelenting focus, and the drastic measures they would take, placed everything they had in jeopardy, but yet I'm asking *them* to help make *your* journey a little less risky?

With everything on the line, it was now do or die. No

time to waste, no skimping or cutting corners. Plan B's weren't even an option. These individuals would now pull every plug, and against the raging current, would paddle for dear life. But yet, I am asking *them* to teach *you* how to stay afloat?

Three quarters of the capacity is sold come the day before their show, and on the day of... a line begins to form outside the club. They stand at the door as the last few people are clicked in, and in disbelief look to the club's owner for confirmation, and his smile does just that. ... They've Sold Out! And now I want *them* to tell *you*, how they did it!

Well, like I said, it took a whole lot of nerve for me to even ask, and though I was truly hoping they would agree to help, I still prepared for the rejection, and many unfortunately I did receive, except for these seven. Not only did these fine individuals agree to help out, they immediately began to tell their story, and though I wanted so bad to sit there and just listen to these incredible journeys that could easily fill their own book, I knew I had to stop them, because I needed them to do it for mine!

So why, after all that they've been through, the money lost, sleepless nights, and stressful weeks, would any of them even consider sharing? Who were *their* mentors, and what books did *they* have to help? There were none!

You see, successful people understand that it takes a

whole lot more than just some advice. That it takes hard work, persistence, and of course passion, because without those three keys, no amount of information or advice will ever help. So with that said, I would like to personally thank the following mentors for not only their generosity, but also for the contribution they've given to the Freestyle genre itself, and if they had ever felt that no one would ever truly understand what they went through, well, now they do, and forever will, because that's what books do!

Mind you, Mentors may have opposing opinions, and none should be considered right or wrong. These individuals combined, represent many years in the business, and their different locations and views should deemed extremely valuable, so come on... Let's Meet The Mentors!

James Rios - Austin, TX.

I have been in the industry for 22 years now and have been promoting shows for 18 of them. It took me four years of watching and learning before I pulled the trigger on my first show. I am glad I did, because I benefited from watching those who did it before me.

I can honestly say that I have blessed to be a part of many successful shows but the one show that sticks out and always will, is the S.A.L. Show at Paradox Nightclub in Austin, TX. This show was something new that had never been done before. It was the ultimate trio Lil Suzy, Lisette

Melendez, and Angel of the original Cover Girls. Each of them would sing their hits with the others singing backup. Well to make a long story short we put 3,300 people in a venue whose capacity was only 808. We had to open our adjoining venue to accommodate everyone. The total cost of that event at the time was approximately $8,500, and we made over $75,000. And that was on a Sunday night in Austin, Texas!!!!

JI Starr - Jersey City, NJ.
I've been promoting moderate sized nightclubs for over 33 years, and the most I probably made in one night was about $7,500.00

Charlie Rodriguez -Miami, FL.
I've been in th business for about 35 years, and am still throwing Freestyle events. So far, the most I've ever made in one night was $160,000.

Hassan Martinez -San Jose, CA.
I have been promoting for 29 years, next year marks my 30th anniversary. The reason I became a promoter is because I got tired of calling clubs and venues to hire me to DJ, so I decided to just throw my own events and invite my favorite DJs to spin with me. By throwing my own events I was able to build a fan base as we were the only promoters spinning Dance, hip hop and Freestyle at the time, definitely influencing the scene in San Jose, California.

The most money I have made in one night was just recent, but my most memorable money making show was my first big show in 1988. It featured JJ Fadd, Dino, Tolga, Stevie B, and the Quickstyle Freestyle dancers. We rented the San Jose Convention Center for the first time and I needed 20k to make it work. Thank God the D boys in the hood who loved my hustle, lent me the cash to make it happen! It was a successful event and the start of a new beginning for me as I was now a "real" event producer..... We grossed a little over $70,000 that night and from there I kept rolling it over to produce more events.

Chuck Lamagra - Rochester, NY.

I have been in the promotions business for 26 years. I started off handing out flyers for a nightclub called Heaven back in 1990. We started bringing in Freestyle acts every Thursday night. Back then all of the acts were on the radio so I took them to do the interviews which helped to promote the shows. The best show I ever did alone was with a few reality show stars from MTV. We grossed over $30,000. I was also involved with a group that co-promoted the American Idol LIVE shows in the Northeast. Each one of those tour stops grossed on average of over $125,000 Man I wish I was solo on those.....6 stops x $125k All in one month!

Luis Pinto - Providence, RI.

I've been putting on Freestyle shows in and around Rhode Island since around 1987, and the most I remember pulling in for myself, in just one night was about $22,000.

Nick Huminski - Chicago, IL.

I've been promoting for 25 yrs., I started out as a music producer and after seeing that the club promoters were making more money than the Artist I decided to give promoting a shot. My very first event was in 1987. I had a large night club and was super excited to do my very first event. In the 80's social media didn't exist. We would print out thousands of posters and flyers and cover the entire city with them. The night of one of my events there was a huge snowstorm, where over seven inches of snow fell. I was devastated. People in those days didn't come out to parties in the snow let alone, a snowstorm. I remember standing at the door thinking to myself this event is going to flop "why did it have to snow today of all days?" I promoted the event for two months canvasing the entire city 12 hours a day, so for this to happen to me was devastating. However, over 700 people showed up for the event and I made $2,000.00 for the night. My very first lesson in promotion was to work hard and don't stop. It was that type of work ethic that got me through the event. I would say that besides the money I made, I also learned a valuable lesson. What you put into a promotion, is what you will get out of it. And as the saying goes... No pain No Gain!

INTRODUCTION

STEP #1 THE BOOKING AGENT - Find out why this particular person will be your most valuable player

STEP #2 FUNDING YOUR EVENT - They'll be begging to give you their money.

STEP #3 CHOOSING THE CLUB - They need you, more than you need them!

STEP #4 CHOOSING THE RIGHT ARTIST – Accessible! Affordable! Accommodating! Perfect! That is the Freestyle Artist!

STEP #5 PROMOTING YOUR EVENT - As long as you keep selling, they'll keep buying.

STEP #6 SHOWTIME - There's no time, like show time, except This Time, its Your Time,

STEP #7 LET'S DO IT AGAIN - The only time you will truly lose, is when you decide to quit!

CLOSING

FREESTYLE

PROMOTIONS
and The 7 Simple Steps
to Getting Started

INTRODUCTION

A banquet hall with a capacity of five hundred people that sold out at $20.00 a ticket just grossed $10,000 for the night. A nightclub with a capacity of fifteen hundred people sells out at $25.00 a ticket just grossed $37,500. An amphitheater with a capacity of three thousand people sells out at $30.00 a ticket just grossed $90,000. And last but not least, an arena with a twenty thousand seat capacity sells out a concert with a $50.00 Ticket just grossed One Million Dollars! And though those numbers are a bit hypothetical, they are in fact accurate enough to get an idea of where I might be going with this book.

Assuming that I now have your attention, it's clear, there's a lot of money involved in promotions, but like any business that promises big rewards, it too has to have its share of risks. Before we move on, or even get excited, please note that I used the term "Gross" which means "Before expenses." In other words, it's going to cost you *some* money to make *that* money, and depending on how that part of the business is handled will determine what we get to take home, or as it's called... Net.

The goal of this book is to try and reignite the spark that many of our Freestyle promoters once had. To give them encouragement, and a few ideas to help them take it to the next level. It is also to help inspire new promoters, to step in and bring to our genre a new and much needed energy. If you're familiar in any way with the Freestyle Music genre you might see it differently than I do. It's very possible that you might see it as a sort of limited genre, if not all together, dead! Well, I'm here to tell you, that Freestyle is still alive and kicking, and maybe I can help inspire you to consider becoming a part of this incredible genre.

I myself have been a part of the Freestyle Music scene for well over twenty-five years. I've worked with the best of the best, and have experienced firsthand both its successes and its failures. Yes, I'm sure that there are many other genres that you can come up with that can be a lot more rewarding, and so can I, but what I am trying to get through to you with this book is, no matter what genre of music you yourself enjoy, if you want to break into the promotions game, Freestyle might just be the best place to start.

Sure the Rap industry has practically taken over the world, but trying to break into *that* circle will without doubt be a dire task. Yes, it's reward is significant, but so is it's risk. The fees to book many of those artists are so outrageous, that they totally eliminate clubs and small venues from even being considered, and this my friends is why Freestyle makes the absolute most sense.

You see with this music, you're dealing with a genre that, though it may be considered old school, new material is still being produced. What this says is that even though the Freestyle heart beats weak, it beats nonetheless, and what I'm hoping this book will do is inspire new blood to flow through its veins so that its heart can once again beat strong.

I'm a booking agent, and an artist manager, and I've seen it all. The ups and the downs, and everything in between, and to me the ups are still so very vibrant, and that is the side I'd like to focus.

By allowing me to show you the potential that Freestyle still offers and helping you to structure it for your own benefit, and the benefit of the genre as a whole would be a great justice to the entire Freestyle community.

In this book you will find some great tips, tricks and techniques, that I hope will help place you on the right path toward a successful career in promotions. The added beauty to it all is that you can take everything you get from this book and apply it to other genres.

Whether that'd be Rap, Rock, Pop and even Latin, this book will certainly help you lay the foundation needed to get started.

However, my deep underlining wish is that you find within these pages a different light. One that shines on the genre of which this book highlights, and that of course would be Freestyle. It began as the music of the Urban Latino, like myself. But it has since grown to reach further. Its universal theme is that of love, a language that every human being on the planet should understand.

At the end of this book is a blank page for you to take notes, and I will advise you to do just that. In fact, I advise you to also write on the pages, fold them and highlight them. Do whatever needs to be done, so that you can absorb the information inside, and hopefully build from there! And when that day comes, that you and I get to finally work together, I want to see this book, and what it was that you did to because so successful. And be ready. I might just ask you to be a part of my next.

Background

I've done just about everything you can think of when it comes to the Freestyle industry. From Writing to productions, marketing to distribution, promotions, label owner, road manager, manager, radio entrepreneur, and of course Booking Agent which eventually became my primary business.

I've worked with every A-List Freestyle Artists you

can name, with an emphasis on a few that I've personally handled, such as Lil' Suzy whom I've worked with since she was just five years old, Angel The Original CoverGirl who I relaunched as a solo act, and then made her part of another package I created in 2004 called S.A.L. a stage concept that consisted of Lil' Suzy, Angel OCG, and Lisette Melendez.

In 2008 I produced the first ever Freestyle Music Awards, a spectacular Star Studded ceremony held in Miami Florida, an event yet to be matched by any. At the awards I introduced my own Men's fragrance called Freestyle by La', a venture that though it didn't flourish as I had hoped, I am still very proud of.

During this time I was also penning my first novel, Freestyle For Life, which became a hit within the Freestyle community, and which I'm certain will one day be considered a Cult Classic. That book was followed by my second novel called Feastyle, where the incredible Lil' Suzy donned it's cover as the Vampiress, Layla Storm.

I've also had the honor of working closely with Tony, Angel, and Aby, the original members of who I consider to be Freestyle's greatest boy band, TKA.

In 2011, I reunited Freestyle's ultimate Girl group, The Cover Girls, and not just three originals, but rather all four including Caroline, Margo, Sunshine, and of course the lead voice behind the hits, Angel.

For over twenty five years I have been operating as a Booking Agent under the La' Entertainment brand and due to my extensive Artist roster, I've been able to service most of the country, and abroad.

I began booking acts in the very early 90's and my travels with then Lil' Suzy, put me face to face with many of the promoters whom I still till this day continue to service.

Lil' Suzy had gained a huge following on the West Coast, mostly in the Bay Area of California. Other huge markets for her included, Illinois, Florida, Michigan, Boston, Arizona, New Mexico, Texas and of course New York's Tri-State area.

It was trips to these markets that introduced me, not just to a whole other fan base that I never knew existed, but also other artists that had I not traveled as extensively as I did, I also would never have known about. Acts such as, Jocelyn Enriquez, Angelina, Rochelle, Spanish Fly, Debbie Deb, L.A.W., Trinere, Freestyle, and others. Acts that had very little presence in the NYC Tri-State area, but were huge everywhere else.

I found myself in a really weird place, not realizing that later on it would pay off greatly. Not only was I meeting these artists, I had the rare opportunity to watch them perform on their own turf, and got to experience firsthand just how popular they really were, though It was still a bit difficult trying to cross

West coast acts into the East and Vice Versa. As far as I was concerned, both sides were missing out big time. It wasn't until I picked up an account with Golo Entertainment who were at the time, representing Low Rider Magazine, that I would get the opportunity to reintroduce certain acts into new areas. I say *Re*-introduced because there was a time that these acts *were* being played on the radio in these markets, but for whatever reason, that was no longer the case.

Low Rider was a great challenge, and due to the nonexistence of Social Media, I really had to go to work to find a lot of these artists.

I had a pretty good relationship with the main promoter, and he and I would brainstorm names that might work. Those he wasn't familiar with, I would actually play their music over the phone, sometimes even sing it myself. Stop laughing!

Between that and the promoter's own research, we came up with a pretty extensive list of acts, many of them I had yet to establish any relations, but as most would guess, that all changed!

Quite a few of the artists on his list included some of the Classic Hip Hop acts such as Rob Base and Doug E Fresh, which opened a whole other area that would also benefit me later on.

In no time I was booking acts such as Lisa Lisa, Stevie B, Doug E Fresh, Rob Base, Lil' Suzy, Angel

OCG, and so many more, not to mention it was at one of these Low Rider events, held in Indiana where I first introduced S.A.L. to about eight thousand people. It was the girl's first show as such, and they not only pulled it off, they killed it! It was then that S.A.L. became Freestyle's newest and hottest act. Everyone wanted them, and actually, still do!

Word spread quickly, not just about this new kid that was booking acts, but more importantly about this new kid that was booking acts for more money than they'd seen in years! Especially those East Coast artists.

During this time, I was working at one of the most popular Freestyle labels in the country, Metropolitan Records. My boss gave me the okay to work my agency right from the Metropolitan office. I guess he didn't think it would really go that far, in fact, neither did I. But in no time, La' Entertainment was on it's feet and running fast, so fast in fact, that I had to make a choice! Stay at Metro, or put it all into La'? And thanks to Angel OCG, who I had already begun dating, and with her trusty Pros and Cons list... was I able to make my decision. And a great decision it was! In no time my home office was up and ready to go, now all I needed was the phone to start ringing, but it wouldn't, and without the security of that steady Metropolitan paycheck, I was getting pretty nervous, and my hopes were starting to crumble, but thanks again to this incredible and supportive person who I was now living with, Angel held down the fort, and created for me a worry-free environment as if she knew that that was all it would take, and before we knew it, the phone began to ring, and hasn't stopped yet!

Word spread quickly, and before I knew it some of my favorite Freestyle artists were calling me direct, asking if I could help them get shows. I got to know many of them, and I listened carefully to their concerns regarding their current situation. I knew what Lil' Suzy was getting, because I was instrumental in getting it, so when I heard what some of these other acts were getting, I was baffled. How were they even surviving? I could understand the female acts, because most of them were married to working husbands, but what about the guys who were expected to take care of their families? And not only was the money a bit insulting, the shows were few and far between.

I didn't realize it then, but I was about to interfere with a system that had been set in motion for several years now. I realized it when two of the most prominent Freestyle Booking Agents out of New York City surprised me with a three-way phone call.

At first I was excited, hearing from these two individuals whom I truly admired and looked up to, as their names were just as iconic as some of the artists of which they represented. I figured they heard about what I was doing and all the shows I had popping off around the country that maybe they wanted to join forces, that would've been amazing, but that wasn't the reason for the call at all, in fact, it wasn't even a nice call... Little did I know, I was about to be scolded!

According to them, I had been making their jobs difficult, and the careers of these artists whom I thought I was doing good by, I was in fact, jeopardizing, maybe even destroying. Well, at least according to them!

You see, my promoters outside of the New York City area knew and respected the artists. They made offers that were respectable, covered their flights and hotels, had limousines pick them up at the airports, and they promoted the way an artist should be promoted, and it worked out great. The shows were successful, and the artists had a great time. It was a win win for everyone! But according to my telephone buddies, that wasn't the case at all. What they said was, I was causing problems!

Apparently, artists whom I had been booking were coming back to New York demanding more money for their performances, creating an uproar among the promoters. No one knew what was happening, until finally, my name came up. "You're screwing up the market!" One of them said, as I sat there trying to make sense of it all. "And you'll be held personally responsible when no one wants to book them anymore!" The other added.

It was suggested that I pull out of the bookings business altogether, and focus on keeping my job at Metropolitan. Then they hung up... Not even a goodbye!

I didn't know what to do, and I had no reason to doubt them, as my experience as an agent couldn't even put a dent into theirs.

I was still processing the subliminal warnings when one of them called me back, but this time, presenting to me what he so boldly referred to as "The perfect solution!"

"Latif," He began. "These artists that you're booking, I can get them for a lot less than what you are getting them, so why don't we do this? You sell the acts to your buyers, but then book them all through me. I can rewrite the deal under my own contract for what I get them for, and you and I can split the difference! Not only that, we can still take fifteen percent for booking.

I could hear his sinister smile right through the phone, and I didn't know what to say.

He gave me a day to think about it, and when he called back the next morning, I respectfully declined his offer. I wanted to explain my reasoning, but the loud clang from when he hung up on me, cut me off mid-sentence.

Why I Wrote This Book

I've always wanted to be a part of something that could somehow change the world. Make people's lives a little easier, a little happier, and maybe even make a couple of dollars in the process.

I knew it had to be something that I was passionate about, because I would want to dedicate myself to it wholeheartedly.

I love the arts, music in particular, and I have a special connection with Freestyle and for obvious reasons of course. But aside from my regular job as a manager and booking agent, which benefits only a select few. I wanted something that had a wider appeal. Something that didn't sway too far from what I already did for a living, and as I kept this at the forefront of my mind for literally years, one day, as I sat in my office staring at the phone that hadn't rung for about a week. I found myself questioning the future of Freestyle music, and then realized something. Though I had shows booked with practically every Freestyle promoter in the country, business was still slow, therefore it wasn't that I wasn't getting the work, because I was. The problem was that there wasn't enough work out there to begin with, and as elementary as that might seem now, at the time, it was an epiphany!

I pulled out this list of contacts that I had compiled over the years, and started reaching out to promoters who I hadn't heard from in a while. There were quite a few, more than what I had even imagined. I didn't want to waste time trying to get them to book acts, because most of them had totally left the business, but what I wanted to know was... What happened? Why'd they stop?

The first several calls were pretty lengthy as these were people who I always got along with, so of course a bit of cordial catching up was to be expected, but at that rate, I'd be on this all week. So the calls got shorter, and the conversations, right to the point, and though most of us would've already guessed the answer, there was nothing like hearing it straight from the promoter's mouth. And yes, the answer was... They could no longer fill clubs.

And though you might feel that the answer was too obvious, truth of the matter is, it wasn't. People not filling clubs may have been the problem, but the cause of that problem was deeper than what any of those promoters cared to even consider.

When I was done with the calls I sat back and gave it all some serious thought. I knew the problem didn't stem from any sort of extinction of the Freestyle fans as a few promoters suggested, because everywhere major concerts were promoted, thousands would show up.

The conclusion I came to was that the spark that once ignited these promoters, didn't burn as it once did. Many of them couldn't even recall how they packed them in the beginning, such as with their unrelenting guerrilla-style tactics, which they worked practically 24/7. People who didn't even know what the hell Freestyle was, ended up at their shows, because that's how these promoters did it. Not a moment went by that they weren't telling someone about their event, and not only did they themselves stand outside clubs to hand out their own flyers, with each hand out also came a pitch. Their flyers saturated trains and parked cars, and any of the business areas close by were paid visits during the lunch hours.

But after several successful events, they thought that was it, they were in, no need to go hard like they used to. Their regular orders of ten thousand flyers shrunk to five thousand, and they no longer hit the streets themselves, but instead gave that most important job to a bunch of untrustworthy kids, many who would simply toss their entire stack of flyers into the trash. This was the beginning of the end, and slowly but surely the crowd would lighten, until finally, the place was empty, and to save face all the promoter could do was point blame at someone, anyone, when all along the only place they should've been pointing... was at the mirror!

It wasn't the market after all. The fans were still fans,

and they still wanted to go out. The artists still had the hits, and still wanted to perform. But the person in between the two, the promoter. *He* stopped. He stopped being excited! Stopped being innovative! He became scared to take risk, and put himself in this little corner where he felt it was safe. He would pick those two or three artists that did well for him, and basically rotate them over and over, until people were tired of seeing them, which proved even more, that it wasn't the artists, nor the fans. It was the promoter, he ceased to promote, and instead relied on hope. He hoped they would come!

So in my opinion, part of the solution would be to try and reignite that old spark within these promoters. Or, would it make more sense to just find *new* ones?

The latter seemed to make the most sense as they could not come with any old Freestyle baggage. They would have to come clean and untainted. No negative experiences allowed! And if they could approach this as a real business, I believe that they could play a huge role in resuscitating this genre. On the flip side however, if they're clean and untainted, then there's a possibility that they wouldn't know enough about the genre to be of any use. I don't know about anyone else, but in order for me to effectively sell something, I have to either be a fan of it, or at the very least, knowledgeable. And that's where the idea for this book came into play.

Who's more knowledgeable about this genre than a fan? Who else has the experience of being lured to an event through some type of marketing, whether that be word of mouth, flyers, radio and so on? Who's walking through the front door of club and concert events more than anyone? So in all actuality, who better than a fan to adopt the role of a Freestyle Club Promoter?

But how would that even happen? What could possibly entice a fan to jump over to the other side of the fence? Money isn't always a good one, because there are much easier ways of making money, and with a lot less risk, and besides, what do fans know about promoting? Who would teach them? Other promoters? What would be in it for them? In fact, what promoter in their right mind would even consider helping out a potential competitor?

And then it hit! What if *I* could teach them? I mean, I've been around long enough and have seen literally thousands of shows go from just an idea to a sold out event. What don't I know about promoting? In fact, I believe my perspective is a unique one, as I observe from a platform unlike anyone else's.

As a Booking Agent, I am usually the first, if not one of the first to know that an event is even in the works, therefore I get to not only *watch* it develop into either a hit or a failure, most of the time, I'm also involved!

Failed events are never good for my business, so when

it does happen I'm concerned, and need to know why? Why did this happen? Whose fault was it? What could've been done to prevent it? Many times this is the discussion I'm having with the promoter, and together we sometimes are able to figure it out, and though it might be too late for that event. It's usually just in time for the next!

It is then up to the promoter whether or not he or she has the stomach to try it again. Many do, but a few don't, and I can't blame them, this isn't for everyone. But those who do hang in there, study their past, and then make the necessary corrections, are eventually going to succeed. That's just the nature of any business.

As the agent, my opinion is constantly sought, and in all honesty, I usually have an answer, and it's because of the thousands of events that I have been a part of. I've seen these promoters first hand. The best of the best, and the worst of the worst.

So I would like to take my experience. The things I've seen and heard. Both good and bad and try and share them with you!

Being a promoter is an incredible job. It has so many great perks, that it can seem way too good to be true, but it's not, and I feel more people should at least give it a try. Let's face it, it's a business like any other business, and not everyone is going to be successful. But you'll never know unless you give it a shot.

Look, if this book could somehow inspire new promoters, it'll benefit so many people. More work for artists, more bookings for the agents, more drinks at the bar, and of course, more shows for the fans to enjoy. The promoters who decide to take this on will have improved their own lives and the lives of their families, as some of those, end of the night payoffs can be quite lucrative. More lucrative than many of your typical 9 to 5s.

So as I mentioned earlier, I want to be a part of something that could change the world, make people's lives a little easier, a little happier, and maybe even make a couple of dollars in the process. Well folks, I truly believe this is it, and I hope that you do too!

Why Freestyle?

You can ask a hundred different people and you will get a hundred different answers, and if you ask me, I'm sure some will agree, and others won't.

New York City was always a melting pot of ethnicity, but the ghetto's during the 70's were populated by mostly African Americans, and Puerto Ricans. The Puerto Rican kids were usually 2nd or 3rd generation Americans, whereas their parents or grandparents came straight from the Island. My mother for instance was born in PR, but raised in Manhattan since infancy.

Growing up we didn't have many influences. The Latin bands were usually much older than us and therefore we couldn't really relate. Our parents and grandparents listened to those bands which immediately made them corny to us. A lot of us also grew up fans of groups like The Jackson Five, The Supremes, and The Osmond Brothers, but for the Latino kids, it was a bit difficult to relate.

The same went on with TV and Movies. We didn't have our own so we borrowed everyone else's. Our Latino Stars were Chico from Chico And The Man, and Julio from Sanford and Son. We related to What's Happening because like Raj many of us were raised by just our mothers, and we watched Good Times because we were familiar with the Ghettos and living in the Projects. Shows like the Brady Bunch were stories of families we were curious about. We were able to go into their homes and see how *they* lived.

When the 80s rolled around we were introduced to Menudo, and though nearly every Puerto Rican girl in New York City fell madly in love with them, every boy hated their fucking guts. After growing up with the Jackson's and the Osmond's, these guys were considered even cornier than the groups our parents liked. We didn't want to associate with them in any way. It was kind of intimidating though trying to talk to a girl while her favorite Menudo member smiled up from the huge button pinned to her chest.

As Latinos we were born showmen, music pumped through our veins since birth, and we danced as if it was second nature. We were sometimes loud and obnoxious, usually one of the class clowns, but only because we loved the spotlight and the attention that came with it and if no one was going to put us up on their stage, then we would build one of our own.

We were great imitators! We mimicked our favorite stars regardless of whether they were singers, dancers, actors or comedians. We had the natural ability to hold a crowd and we did just that. Whether it was in school, on the block, or at home in front our family.

We all knew people who were musicians. Titi played the Organ, and Tio played the Guitar. Our parents took us to Central park and Randalls Island where the teenagers and young adults smoked weed and played the Congas. It was an open jam session for all who wanted in. You could bring your own Conga, maracas, or tambourine, and if you didn't have any of those, you could just clap your hands in a swinging rhythm and you were in.

This was the music that we grew up on, these were the sounds and rhythms, so of course the moment we had an opportunity to create our own, it was bound to sound similar, But what about those beats? You mean those beats that we learned to rap to? They inspired us to tell a story, and if it was just the beat, then I could understand our lyrics being a bit more rugged. But it wasn't. Our music was melodic, and soulful, giving it that softer edge. Our music never made you feel like going out and looking for trouble. Instead, it made us want to go out and look for love!

It went by names such as Latin Hip Hop, Latin Dance, High Energy, Heartthrob, Latin Freestyle and so on. Today we just call it Freestyle, and even acts who may have at one time been considered Pop Artists, are now better known as Freestyle Artists, thanks to the many concerts that labeled them as such. And though some might consider it a dying genre, or already dead, I certainly don't. Stagnant? Yes! Lacking of growth? Absolutely! But dead? No, not at all! And until Freestyle is able to once again find its way, I will do whatever *I* possibly can, to sustain its life, and protect its integrity. Hey, Freestyle Music derived from the Urban Latino Youth of New York City, and whether we acknowledge it or not, it has become a sort of nucleus to our culture, and I feel, that in order to preserve our culture, then our music too must be preserved.

The Audience

Many of our originators didn't come into the music because they were fans of it, because at the time, the genre as we know it, didn't even exist. They just did what they naturally loved. They produced the music that felt right, and wrote the stories they wanted to tell. They sang in a tone that was most comfortable, and wore outfits that expressed who they were. This was Freestyle before we even knew what Freestyle was, and I believe that the first Freestyle fans ever, were the artists themselves.

Each artist became a sort of role model for the next, which is probably why many are so similar. Finally, we found stars that we can relate to, and call our own, some even looked like us. And of course they did, they were Latinos.

Just about everyone who saw a performance became inspired to do the same. Some actually pulled it off, and those who didn't tried their hand in other areas such as writing, producing, and even dancing.

Deejays became crucial element in the success of the genre, and it was through them that we were able to get our music to the masses. Freestyle wasn't the blues, it was love music, happy music. Music about crushes, falling in love, promises and hopes. Once in a while there'd be a song about heartbreak, but even in those we were able to find comfort.

Back then falling in love was a big deal among teenagers, and many Freestyle songs were claimed as the theme to their lives. I also believe that Freestyle songs have more titles with the word love in it than any other genre.

Many of our artists originated from the ghettos of

New York City. Starting from The Bronx, Manhattan, and so on. They resembled the guys and girls that lived next door to us. That we sat next to in class, or would run into at the supermarket or the handball courts. They were Latino kids that we fell in love with, and what topped it all off was, they were accessible.

They became more than just people whose songs we loved. They became our representatives, and their music, our common language. It formed a community of like mindedness. If a particular Freestyle act was performing somewhere, we knew what to expect when we got there. We knew what kind of people were going to be in the audience and there was something special about that.

The fan base began to expand. First with a variation of Latinos, from Puerto Ricans, to Cubans, Colombians and Mexicans. They took on different skin tones, from the darkest of dark, to the palest of pales, and the diversity was not only adding to the beauty of our landscape, it was also opening it up to an even wider fan base.

Though we adore the music, it's important to keep in mind, that behind it all, there lies a business, and like any business, if mismanaged, it will surely suffer, and that it did!

Many of those involved behind the scenes really had no business being there in the first place. I'm not talking about the actual talent. I'm talking about those so-called executives who just happened to be in the right place at the right time. They had no real experience, and hiring a professional to come in and help run things the way they should, to them made no financial sense whatsoever. And we can't really blame the artists, all they wanted to do was sing!

And just as fast as the genre took off, it would land. Many of the acts, turned off by the way things were handled decided to step away. Groups split, managers got fired, and producers and DJs tried switching genres. It was a devastating blow for Freestyle, and the only ones who seemed to have found the silver lining were those acts who had yet to establish themselves, totally ignoring the fact that the reason they never made it in the first place was simply because... They just weren't that good!

Thanks to the introduction of Home Studios, the days of high priced recording sessions were no longer the only choice, and the consumer manufacturers of cassette tapes and Cd's weakened the dependency artists had on the major record companies.

Independent was no longer a dirty word, in fact, it now carried a whole new meaning, and many of the Freestyle artists found within it a brand new home, along with a brand new hope!

Anything that was, or is popular, at one time began within a niche market. That niche most likely catered to a small and particular demographic. Music is the greatest example I know, for each genre of it began by catering to just a few. It spoke to their hearts, and reflected their lives. In time, those genres would reach further, speaking to even more hearts and reflecting even more lives, until the walls that separated each came crashing down.

Freestyle music shares that same history. As a music that once catered to the Urban Latino Youth of New York City, it eventually found itself in the hearts of others. Different races and ethnicities took to Freestyle as if it had been created specifically for them, and it was, it just took a little longer to get there.

Love is something that we all share. Its God's first gift to us, even before life itself, proved by the deep affection a mother displays toward her child who's still in the womb. So why wouldn't Freestyle Music cater to the masses? It's about love, something every single one of us could relate.

The point that I am trying to get through here is the fact that everyone is a potential attendee to your Freestyle event, and therefore no stones should be left unturned. Every street of every city, walks a possible audience member, and though I would encourage you to really streamline your marketing efforts, I just want to make sure that you don't ignore anyone, because you really never know!

I for instance, live in a tiny town in North Caroline.

Yet, I am one of Freestyle's primary Manager / Agents, and my wife is the incredible lead singer of one of Freestyle's greatest girl groups. As of this writing we've already been here over ten years, and we've met many people.

A typical conversation in everyday life usually includes some sort of inquiry about your occupation. It's not out of noisiness, just part of good ol' getting to know you! Not to mention, for some people, their occupation actually defines them.

My wife and I don't usually volunteer information about what we do for a living, but if it comes up, we don't dismiss it, nor do we lie. We're proud to talk about it, taking precaution not to come across boastful or braggart, as the nature of our wonderful careers can indeed strike up a bit of envy.

When asked what kind of music we do, we tell them Freestyle, prepared to go into a bit more detail, as we do not expect anyone out here to know much, if anything at all about it.

That was typically the case. However we've been noticing a change. Not only are the people from around here familiar with the music, many we're finding out, are actual fans.

One person in particular was this young kid who had just started working at the barbershop where I get my cut. He was pretty skillful, so one day my regular barber was on vacation so I let him cut my hair because I had a show that weekend.

And like most sessions, it came with a pretty cool conversation where we sort of got to know each other, and I anticipated the inevitable question, about what I did for a living.

I usually don't say booking agent because people don't always know what that is, confusing it sometimes with a Bookie, two totally different jobs. I use the term talent agent, and then add to it, "I book talent to perform at club and concert events around the country." This is usually followed by another question, which is, "Anyone I might know?"

I begin by saying that the type of music I'm involved with is called Freestyle, but this time, just as I was about to break it down, this kid flinched and gave me a strange look.

He stopped cutting and looked at me through the mirror and said, "I fucking love Freestyle!" Immediately I assumed that he was confusing it with Freestyle Rap, and was about to clarify, when I nearly fall out of the chair when he continued with; "I've been in love with Lil' Suzy for years..."

I knew he didn't get the information from my regular barber because we've never talked about it, not to mention, my barber didn't even speak English. It wasn't because of the color of his skin either, because Freestyle tore down that barrier years ago. It wasn't even because he was from this little town in North

Carolina. It was because of his age. The kid was younger than my own son, who though was raised in a Freestyle household, has absolutely no interest in the genre. I was baffled! My skepticism forced me to throw in a few more test, but to this kid they weren't test at all, just two people talking about a passion they both share.

Of course, I had to ask him about The Cover Girls, where he simply replied by singing the hook to Show Me, and at that very moment, as if the whole thing had been staged, in walks my wife who was next door getting her nails done... He recognized her immediately!

I find this story extremely fascinating, and I mention it here because I want to make a point. You see, we can't predict who the fans are anymore. Doesn't matter what they look like, where they're from, or even how old they are, so don't sleep on anyone, and realize also that the music that might be Old School to us, can be brand new to someone else, and just as we became fans, so can anyone, whether it was back in the day, or tomorrow.

Nowadays towns such as where I live, no longer host a majority of native residents. With Military relocation, affordable travel, reliable vehicles, and now the Internet, families can sit in front of their computers, and with just a few clicks, choose where they would like to live the rest of their lives.

So when I speak about the audience, it can't be geared toward race and ethnicity, because in all honesty, that really doesn't apply anymore. Age however might make a bit more sense, and even those lines, as I proved with the story of the barber, also, may no longer apply.

Therefore, you must eliminate all prejudices, and re-approach marketing with a clean slate, and restructure your very own demographics according to where you intend to start promoting. You just might be pleasantly surprised by who ends up walking through that door.

The Fairest Deal

As a Booking Agent I stand dead center between the artists and the promoters. Whereas each side strives to get for themselves the better deal, I on the other hand strive to get the fairest. A deal where both sides walk away happy and satisfied, because a successful event is one we can all celebrate.

I've seen with my own eyes just how strong this genre can be. I've seen some incredible turnouts, but I've also seen some embarrassing ones.

I'm the person that both sides feel most comfortable confiding in. If either artist or promoter has a bad experience, I'm usually the first to know. And while others would probably just wave it off as just another complaint, I listen carefully, because usually, they're both right, just that their communication is a bit screwed up, which is where I come in. I'm able to take in their individual concerns, and then try and represent them in a way that makes sense to both. And so far, I've been pretty successful.

It's as simple as understanding and addressing the problems early on, and from there, trying to come up with a solution.

You see, in the beginning, everyone is so focused on doing the deal that they overlook, or sometimes even ignore the details. It's like any relationship, you usually put your best foot forward, but later on, when everyone is relaxed, true colors show, and it becomes a disaster, which not only leads to an unsuccessful event, it also leads to bad experiences, bad blood, and the loss of any possible repeat business.

Promoters have been known to exaggerate and promise things that they never thought through. Things that, when the time came were impossible for them to deliver. Artists also have been known to promise things at the beginning, that they later failed to honor, and sometimes Booking Agents go along just so the gig goes through, because if it doesn't, well... they don't get paid!

There will be many times that a promoter might request services outside of the artist's typical deal. Some of these things might include, autograph signings, meet and greets, special song request, in-stores, and so on, and any agent who just assumes an artist would comply, is setting everyone up for a huge disappointment, if not an all-out disaster.

I've been in situations where certain requests were made, that I knew for sure would be turned down, and would inform the promoter as such, and if it couldn't be worked out, sometimes they'd pick another act.

Then there were those who had their heart set on their ideas and would just pull out altogether. But the worst situation, for me at least, is when the promoter would feel that another agent could do better, and totally abandons my ship for my competitor's. Of course my first instinct is to lose my mind, but what I've learned over the years is to let them go, and with blessings, so when they realize that what they were asking would never happen, they'll return, all because my door was left open for them.

It's risky, because I'm in the business of bookings, and every booking that doesn't go through is a strike against my own pocket. But I've learned that if I could catch these problems at the gate, I could nurture them, and guide the promoter accordingly, usually concluding the event successfully, while most importantly, building relationships that will lead to repeat business for all involved.

The situation works the other way as well. Where new

promoters looking to book, approach me with artists that I feel might cause them some problems, especially for those promoters who are still a bit star struck, which may be cute, but definitely not good for business.

Fanaticism isn't something any promoter wants to display to an artist. Hey, we're all fans in some capacity or another, but we have a job to do, and each job requires a certain amount of control, and if an artist is able to control you, they'll also be a able to control your event, so it's important that if I feel a particular artist isn't a good first choice, you might just want to listen. We're not crossing those artists out permanently; we'll get to them, just not yet.

Look at it this way. The bigger the act the more they cost to book, and the more they cost to book the bigger my commission! So it's totally against my own financial interest to sway you from the big acts, but my goal is long term and so should yours. Believe me, we have plenty of time to pull in the big acts, and if we start off right, we'll get there... I promise!

SIMPLE STEP #1

THE BOOKING AGENT

James Rios: In my 21 years in the industry I have learned that there are certain artists who will only book through an agent and then you will find those greedy ones that will say, " Next time you book call me or my manager directly and we will give you a better price. I will be honest in saying that a few times I did it direct and those were the worst shows I ever did. With a booking agent, you are paying for a peace of mind, knowing the artist will show, when they will arrive, what time they will go on, how long they will perform, and it's all laid out in the contract. When using an agent they will go above and beyond to help because they, just like you want a successful show, not just for you, but for them and the artist. If they fail, who would want to book again? I have been helped out by booking agents in more ways than I could possibly tell you. Yes you will pay a little more for that service but always remember that the grass may be greener on the other side but you always have to pay to keep it that way.

I decided to begin these seven simple steps with what some might consider bias if not altogether shameless coming from me, as my primary position within this industry is that of a Booking Agent.

But the reason wasn't to highlight me or my business,

but rather anyone who operates under the Booking Agent umbrella. Whether they are to me, friend or foe, comrade or competitor, so long as they practice with the integrity and professionalism so important for the survival of our particular field.

Every agent represents every other agent, and together we represent one of the most important, not to mention historical positions in the entertainment industry.

But aside from playing matchmaker between Talent and event, agents are able to provide for their clients, something else. Something much more valuable than just booking, yet many fail to realize, and therefore never take advantage of. So I'm hoping that this chapter sheds a whole new light on the role of the booking agent, and show you just how very important they may be to your new venture as a Freestyle Club Promoter!

The practical experience that comes from the many events that an agent has handled throughout his or her career developed in them a very unique perspective as to the workings of the industry. They stand between two entities, each side presenting demands that oppose the other, yet the agent must somehow create even ground, and bring together the two sides, because when done properly, the success that both stand to gain, can be quite significant.

Booking Agents should always be willing to advise,

and even guide their clients. I personally have worked with so many promoters of whom I've practically taken by the hand and walked through the entire process.

This type of involvement of which I participated has an industry name of its own, it's called consulting, a popular business no doubt, and one whose services can be quite costly, yet I, as a Booking Agent as I'm sure many others, have provided this invaluable service many many times, and absolutely free of charge! Which should now clarify why I made the Booking Agent, Simple Step #1

I tell my kids all the time, "Why learn from your own mistakes, when you can learn from the mistakes of others?" Not that there is anything wrong with mistakes, on the contrary, mistakes are an absolute necessity in business, and in life.

What mistakes tell us is simply this, "Hey, you're doing it all wrong, try it another way!" But in order to hear them, we have to listen, and then act, And though learning from other's won't stop us from ever making our own, it will at least make room for us to make other mistakes, hopefully those needed to get us to where we want to be. I ask a lot of questions, it's just my nature. And I love to learn. I'm fortunate to have worked with some of the best Freestyle promoters in the industry, fascinated by how they each approach their craft, regardless of the fact that their goals are identical. My experience has conditioned me to recognize the steps toward a successful event, as it has also conditioned me to sort of predict its failure. Many times I would speak up, usually with a tip that I might've picked up from another source, but other times it was best to remain silent, as some promoters just aren't interested in anyone else's ideas. But then the inevitable happens, and I saw it coming. Yeah I regret not saying anything, but what was I to do? And now look, it's over, and this promoter took a pretty serious hit, and just as I was able to make that first prediction, my second says, that promoter will never book again! So with that said, I need to come right out and say this, the Booking Agent is without doubt one of the most important people on your team, so treat them as such and take advantage of their unique knowledge and understanding of this business. Not that you have to agree with everything they say, but at least hear them out, you never know, they might just have what you need to get your business over the top, and they're willing to share it with you, absolutely free!

Charlie Rodriguez: *I have used booking agents as well as gone direct to the artists. The advantage of using an Agent is that you make one phone call and they take care of the rest, especially when you're dealing with a new artist. The booking agent also knows when there are competing events occurring at the same time that could compromise yours. I also at times like to go direct with certain artists as after so* *many years working we've become friends. Sometimes we don't even do contracts. Your word is your bond.*

Going Direct

Thanks to the Internet, it's become quite easy to track down and book an artist direct, however, booking an artist from anyone other than a reputable Booking Agent, is like buying a Rolex watch right off the street, though it might seem like you got a great deal, if that watch ever decides to stop working, you're on your own!

An agent normally charges an artist just 10%, and that's only if the deal goes through, and though it's a small price for that peace of mind, not to mention a smooth transaction, struggling artists will still try and oppose it in order to save that booking fee. But for you as the promoter, that move makes absolutely no sense, as that peace of mind should apply to you as well, with the only difference being that you as the promoter, don't have to pay for it. Even if the artist has someone handling their bookings, whether it be a manager, group member, or even another agent, doesn't matter, you as the promoter should be able to use your own chosen agent, if that's what makes you comfortable. And if there *are* two agents involved, don't worry about it, they'll work it out between them.

Luis Pinto: *It makes the most sense to go through a agent, for one it* *makes the entire process easier, not to mention, once you build a relationship with that agent, he's more likely to help find you the best deals.*

In the event that an agent refuses to book a particular artist, it's worth your investment to find out why. If it's due to personal reasons, then that agent should have no problem with you acquiring that artist elsewhere. But if the problem is business, the agent should be honest and explain so that you can make your own decision as to whether or not you should book them. I for one find it very important to give the promoter the complete run down on any artists they might be interested in booking, both good experiences and bad, because if something were to go wrong, I would definitely have to answer some questions. Bad business includes things such as, being rude and uncooperative, poor performance, disrespectful to fans, pulling out of scheduled meet and greets, unnecessary demands, unpreparedness or just plain not showing up. But in defense of the Freestyle genre, I am proud to say, we're dealing with a pretty stable bunch, so most of those scenarios, at least for now, are rare to non-existent. So in closing of this very important topic, let me add this. Don't work harder, work smarter, and get yourself a damn agent!

Nick Huminski: *Booking agents are the bridge between the artist and promoter. It is very important to have a good working relationship with* the booking agent. *Always pay and honor your agreement otherwise your reputation, not to mention your career, may be very short lived.*

The Artist Engagement Contract

What is the contract? What is it for? Who does it benefit? And do we really need it? Booking contracts are one of the most straight forward and simplest contracts to read and understand. This is very important because once a promoter decides to book an act, it is imperative that the booking is quick, clear, and most importantly, safe. There is no time to consult with an attorney, which is why standard contracts are used. Some might argue that there is no such thing as a standard contract, but I disagree. Though some contracts might be adjusted slightly from artist to artist, the bulk of it is pretty much the same. I've been using the same contract for over twenty years, and have absolutely no reason to change it, as it has done exactly what it was created for, and I've never had a problem, not to mention both the artists and promoters that I work with regularly are so accustom to it, that I can bet that neither side even reads it anymore.

To summarize a typical agreement I would say it goes a little something like this. I the promoter agree to pay you the artists for a performance at this place on this date for this amount of money, including these flights, hotels and other... and he signs. And by the artist signing, they agree to provide their performance at this place, on this date for this amount of money! And it really is that simple!

Now there are a couple of add-ons that might or might not follow a contract, and for different reasons. One of those add-ons is called the Terms and Agreement.

JI Starr: When I first started there was a booking agent who was getting over on me with prices, but once I found out and verbally kicked his ass, he apologized and we became very good friends, and believe me, the importance of a good relationship in this business is priceless. I would also at times get exclusives from certain artists who were from around my area, another result of good working relationships.

Unlike the contract that typically takes up a full page, the Terms & Agreement can be two or more. What the Terms & Agreement is, is a more detailed breakdown of the initial contract. It speaks mostly of the liabilities, and who's responsible for what. And if there is a discrepancy, how it is to be handled. I am selective when using Terms & Agreements because I feel it can be quite intimidating. However, if I in anyway feel uncomfortable with a booking, that maybe the promoter might be unclear, I have two choices, either issue a Terms and Agreement, or pass on the deal.

Another Add-on that I deal with a bit more is called the Artist Rider. There are two types of riders, a

Hospitality Rider and a Technical Rider. The Hospitality Rider is something you will usually get when dealing with a more current act, as these riders can be quite extravagant and demanding. I have not only seen many of these Riders, I've at times had to implement them into deals. Some are annoying, obnoxious, and even unnecessary, while others can be quite entertaining. Though Freestyle artists don't normally issue Riders, when they do, they're pretty simple, usually requesting things that they need rather than things they want. A large mirror in the dressing room, plenty of outlets, bottled water at room temperature, maybe a light snack to hold them over until after the show, things like that. The few that I felt were a bit obnoxious and unnecessary were those that asked for stupid things like, Two pounds of M&Ms, absolutely no green ones. A dinner spread in the dressing room that could feed ten people, yet there's only two. Or a bottle of Colonche, a liquor you can only find in Mexico. And though the following requests have yet to cross my desk, I have heard of artists also requesting drugs, and / or personal entertainment.

The other type of Rider is what is called a Technical Rider aka Tech Rider. This sort of add-on agreement is a bit different because it request things necessary for the performance. And though some of these can be quite extravagant, they at least add to the overall show experience. But we're dealing with Freestyle artists, and their tech Riders are pretty simple, usually requesting no more than a wireless microphone, and some way of running their track.

Hassan Martinez: To me it's important to deal with an agent so that I don't have to deal with the madness that sometimes comes with booking an artist. An agent can also recommend artist that may work better in my market, saving me from having to experiment on my own. Oh, and of course, I rather send my money to a trusted agent, than directly to an artist.

Paying The Artist

Once the artist's availably is green lit, the fee is negotiated, and the contract is signed, the next thing that needs to be done is the deposit. Deposits are normally fifty percent of the total artist fee, not including expenses, meaning flights, hotel etc. This deposit is to be sent to the Booking Agent, either by mail via check, money order, bank to bank wire transfer, or if the agent's bank is close by, a direct deposit is always the simplest and cheapest. Keep in mind though, the show cannot be advertised, promoted, or even mentioned without the deposit being made and cleared, and since most promoters want to begin their campaigns immediately wire transfers and direct deposits are usually preferred.

Let's go back for a minute, to the subject about dealing

direct with artists, this is why it can be risky, as no artist will hold a date without a deposit, which means you have to send it to them. So what if that artist fails to make the show? What happens then? Well, you can sue, but if you've ever dealt with Entertainment Attorneys you will know that they are some of the most expensive attorneys in the field, and chances are their fees will cost you a lot more than the deposit you are actually trying to get back, and though a booking agent can easily face a similar situation, that chance is slim to none, for if an agent were to ever release that type of negative information into the marketplace, rest assured that artist's reputation will be wrecked for the remainder of whatever career they might have left.

Chuck Lamagra: *Booking Agents help guarantee that on the day of the show, that the artist shows up, or in the case of an emergency, a suitable replacement.*

Okay, back to Paying The Artists. After the advanced deposit is made, the remaining fifty percent is due upon artist's arrival. This balance will usually be collected by the road manager. Large concerts usually pay at the venue, but always prior to performance. Smaller events, such as club shows usually pay the balance upon check-in at the hotel, or if the show is local, as soon as the artist arrives. Balances are paid in Cash Only, and big bills are always preferred, though unless it's all in singles you won't normally hear any complaints. If it's a multiple act event, it might be a good idea to have the artist or their rep sign something, maybe a receipt book stating that the cash was received. As for how to handle taxes, I would consult with an accountant and see what would work best for your particular situation, as I have personally seen so many variations.

SIMPLE STEP #2

FUNDING YOUR EVENT

James Rios: The very first show I ever did I had to use my entire bank account, savings account, coins, and even pawn a few things for the deposit and plane tickets. Nothing like showing up to the bank with $700 in loose change. If looks could kill I would have been dead. I had to prove that a show would bring revenue before I would get the financial backing that was needed.

What stops most of us from pursuing our dreams, and endeavors, usually has something to do with money. It takes money to make money is how we've been conditioned, and though some of that may be true, most of it isn't.

Yes we need the physical aspect of money to buy the things we need in order to build, but it doesn't necessarily take money to make money. What it takes is innovation, imagination, vision, and persistence. Our brains have been created to tackle the most sophisticated problems on earth, so why can't it tackle a measly money problem? Study those who came before us. Those who started, super companies. You will learn that many of them started out with little to nothing.

One of the reasons why I based this book around the genre of Freestyle music, is because it is, in my opinion, the most affordable genre to present, and whose artist are still popular enough to draw interest. Now notice, I said affordable, not cheap. Cheap isn't always good, as you usually get what you pay for. I say affordable because it will not cost you an arm and a leg... Just a couple of fingers, and if you're smart, those fingers don't even have to belong to you!

Nick Huminski: Funding an event is a multi-faceted situation. In most cases you have to personally fund each event. Nightclubs for instance generally only allow established promoters an opportunity to promote at the venue. If you are not established they will generally give you a weekday to see if you have the ability to draw a crowd, and if you fail, the Club owner will most likely show you the door.

Before you start seeking funds, it's important to first figure out what exactly you would need it for? It's easy to lose track of spending, so be clear on how you intend to spend it.

So where would you get this money to put on an event? Well, here's one idea that you can probably utilize immediately. Bank accounts! Now how easy was that? You've been saving for several years now, accumulating a nice little stash, but what are your plans with it? Buy a house? A car? Take a vacation? Or maybe you've been saving that money to send Junior to college next year? But So what! You'll put it back, right? That Monday morning following your anticipated sold out show, you'll be back at the bank putting it all right back where it came from, along with a little extra from the profits. Oh but wait! You're having second thoughts? I guess that great idea isn't so great after all, especially when it has to do with *your* money!

If you believe so much in your own venture, then the first place you should seek funds is from your own pocket. However, if you don't have the money, then okay, I understand. But please, if you don't believe in yourself, don't expect others to believe in you, it will show clear as day.

So once again, funding your own first event, would be the absolute best investment you'll ever make in this business, because even if you lose money, the knowledge that you'll gain from the process will be invaluable, to every other event afterwards, not to mention your reputation will remain intact, and in good standing for when you finally do approach others to invest. Funding your first event will force you to pay extra attention to detail. It will sharpen your negotiation skills, and teach you which corners to cut, and prepare you in case you have to come to the rescue by trading in some of your own sweat so that your money can go a bit further.

You will never experience *true* entrepreneurialism, until you have built a business with your own hands, and money. Doesn't mean you are not an entrepreneur, but the experience of having your entire being invested into something is an experience unlike anything else.

And for those who just don't have it, where things are so tight, that they could barely keep enough money in the bank to cover its own monthly fee, let alone any significant savings. With no home to mortgage, car, or other assets to help out, they live day to day, and hand to mouth, and the only thing they have to invest are a bunch of dreams, and bright ideas, and that sweat I spoke about earlier. Well, this is the majority, and if you study the entrepreneurs that came before you, the richest and most famous. Those who changed the world, and made lives better, you'll learn that most had nothing but those same dreams and bright ideas that you do.

So how did they fund these ideas? Simple... Through Friends and family!

Hassan Martinez: I wanted to take my parties to the next level and needed money to book an artist. So I had to head to the D Boy homies in the hood for a short loan of 5k. Of course they wanted to be a part of the party. My first artist I ever booked was Cynthia! I wound up selling all the tickets in advance which gave me the credit I needed with the D Boys and they wound up becoming my street promoters.

Asking Family and Friends

Asking friends and family to give you money for an event might be the hardest thing you'll ever do. Not because you're afraid they might say no, but rather afraid that they might actually say yes and now you'll have to deliver, and until then, all eyes will be on you.

One friend or family member can keep every other member from ever giving you anything. You can ask them to keep it between just the two of you, but good luck with that one, because if you screw up, trust me, everyone will know it.

On the other hand, if you're successful, others will be offended that you didn't offer them the same opportunity, a great example of the old "Damned if you did, damned if you don't!"

You have to think long and hard, not whether or not you should go this route, because I think you should. But rather how you should handle each situation, good or bad, because usually when friends and family do agree to invest, it isn't because of the potential return, it's because they believe in you, they love you, and they want to be supportive.

But when they refuse to invest, it isn't always because they're afraid of losing their money, but more so losing the relationship, so you can't take it personal, just move on to the next and rest assure they'll be watching.

So how *should* you handle this? Or better yet, how do you even ask? What do they get back in return? And if they say no, how quickly can you patch the huge hole you just blew in the side of that boat?

The absolute first thing you need to make sure of before you ask anyone for even a cent, is exactly how much money you need, and exactly what you need it for. Nobody is going to feel comfortable just padding your bank account without knowing exactly where their money will go. So whether it's a detailed business plan, or just a financial one, hand them something that they can take home and make sense of.

Charlie Rodriguez: All funding falls on me, and I sign the contracts!

The good thing about doing it this way is that you can actually show them what they themselves invested in. Was it the flyers? The hotel rooms, the flights, or maybe they invested enough to cover the artist. So now even if the event itself failed, they can still account for their investment and doing it this way might actually help keep them investing in future events, even if they take a hit.

Write down the entire process step by step, and at each of those steps, figure out if there's a cost, and if there is, how much? You see the key here is that your financial needs don't have to be presented in bulk.

They can be presented in smaller, more manageable increments, and then distributed to the best person to handle each amount.

Now once you put all those numbers together, and have carefully gone over it, you need to make a list of everyone you know that might be able, and willing to help with something.

For example, your little sister might be able to invest the hundred dollars you need for the graphic designer who will be working on your flyer. Uncle Jimmy might be able book the hotel rooms with his credit card, and Mrs. Robinson from next door might have some frequent flyer miles she isn't going to use this year.

This is what I mean by using your brain, being innovative, and imaginative. It is possible to get what you need, just focus and persevere. The training you'll receive from this will be invaluable, and had you been so fortunate as to have unlimited financial resources, you would have no inclination or motive to challenge yourself, to get the job done by any means, and if you failed, there would be a good chance that you'd never try it again!

Set up a business, at least a Sole Proprietorship to start. That could be obtained through the local county clerk's office. Once you have your business certificate, bring it to the bank and open an account under your business name.

Deposit all investments in full, whether cash or check so that your investors can see where the money is, and later on, how it was used.

Now what about those big ticket investments? For example, artist fees! Well, who says you have to use just one person to invest in that? Look at it this way, how much easier will it be to get ten people to invest two hundred dollars each, than it would be trying to get one person to take on the whole two grand?

So let's talk about the return. Borrowing money is a pretty straight forward process. Someone lends us money and we pay it back, it's really that simple, and when you're dealing with friends and family, that's pretty much the way it's done. However, you're building a business here, and if you don't have your own money, then it's important to at least have access to money, and for many, that means borrowing from friends and family.

Did you know that Motown Record's founder Berry Gordy started his legendary label with an $800 loan from *his* family?

Return On Investment

A loan is a sum of money that is expected to be paid back, usually with interest. And an Investment is a monetary asset purchased with the idea that the asset will provide income in the future or will be sold at a higher price for a profit. In other words, a loan is expected to be paid back regardless, and with interest, and an investment is a buy into a particular business, with a share in both the risk and the reward. So with that said, which do you seek? It's best to know this before approaching anyone because if you aren't a hundred percent clear as to the deal you are offering, they won't be a hundred percent clear about how you intend on paying them back. Regardless as to whether you are dealing with family, friends, or complete strangers, take care of business the right way and you will always have people willing to help you out.

So let's begin with loans because they're much simpler to understand, mainly because most of us have dealt with loans at some point in our lives, whether through a mortgage, car loan, credit card, or just a personal loan from someone you know. When you borrowed, you were expected to pay back and in many cases with interest. The reason there are businesses that offer loans is because it's a big business. These loan companies make a lot of money, the interest paid back can equal more than the original amount borrowed.

It's totally legal to lend money on a private one to one basis, however you must take precaution when charging interest, or accepting collateral because there are limits to how much interest you can charge, and it differs from State to state, so check yours under Usury law, and of course, hiring an attorney to help out, even if it's just to draft your first agreement.

An investment works a bit differently, as the Investor is basically buying either into your company so as to benefit from all events, or buying only into one event where he or she would share with you a percentage of the profits, and if there are no profits then, they too would absorb the loss.

These deals can all be customized to everyone's approval, but again, keep in mind your state laws, and whatever deal you agree to, make sure you put it on paper. It is very easy to misunderstand, or miscommunicate a detail that could land you in court, not to mention a relationship ruined for life.

Sponsors

Chuck Lamagra: For every show I get sponsors that want to be a part of my flyers, posters, social media, and radio ads. This technique once helped pay for everything, before even one ticket was sold.

Companies tend to invest a lot of money into their marketing campaigns. These campaigns may consist of all, or some of the following, Such as Print advertising in Magazines, Newspapers, Flyers, Posters, and Billboards. Radio and Television, Social Media, Publicity where they hire publicist to help feature stories about them in popular medias.

Another huge part of the marketing campaign is

Sponsorship, where the companies pay event promoters to allow them to advertise their products or services to their audiences.

When we think of Sponsors, of course we immediately think of Budweiser, Coke Cola, and other monster corporations. We see their advertisements at all major sporting events, making that idea seem a bit impossible for the small night club promoter.

But just as there are major corporations sponsoring major events, there are also smaller corporations sponsoring smaller events, and that's where you want to go!

So how can we get companies to sponsor our Freestyle events? First off, we have to be clear as to who our audience is? How are they living? Is it mostly male or female? Married, or single? What do they wear, drive, eat and drink? What types of entertainment do they enjoy, and whatever other common interest you can figure out.

Immediately you are going to start connecting these things with the majors, for instance, what do they wear? You might come up with a line of clothing that will be out of your reach, however, what about the small clothing stores that sell that line or maybe a line very similar? Same when it comes to what they're driving, don't go after Ford, but rather the smaller mom and pop car dealers that sell used Fords. You get the idea, right?

Now of course with the Internet you can get sponsors from pretty much anywhere, especially if they are strictly an on-line merchant, but let's not forget about the typical brick and mortar operations, however, when dealing with these establishments it is important to stay within the vicinity. Nowadays we are being bombarded by major retail outlets, therefore those independently owned operations can really use your help, and your event can be just what they were looking for.

Clothing and shoe boutiques, restaurants, gyms, health food stores, Karate schools, car dealerships, dry cleaners etc. You get the idea, and can probably come up with others. These are some of your potential sponsors. Just don't waste time trying to get a Brooklyn store to sponsor your event in Queens.

So who do we approach, and what do you ask for? Well, each situation will be different, because each sponsor is different and what might work for one might not necessarily work for the other, this is where you, the businessperson has to put time and thought into, and trust me, if done right, will be well worth it.

One of the problems I've seen promoters face when approaching potential sponsors. Is that they don't know what to ask. If you don't know what to ask, then sponsors won't know what to give.

Just as we would for investors, we need to lay out the

numbers for the sponsors. Not about how much money you expect to make, their more interested in how many heads you might be able to pull through the door, so you need to project this number, along with how you plan to make that happen.

I've seen major corporations sponsor small events, though it really isn't the norm, so I think you should stay away from them for now, and focus instead on the smaller more manageable businesses and start-ups from around the area, those that can directly benefit from your event.

This would be great training, and once mastered, upgrading to a deal with the big boys will work out a lot smoother.

Unlike the majors, these smaller entities don't usually have departments that handle Sponsorships, so in these cases you'll most likely be dealing directly with the owner!

Just because they're not too familiar with your type of business, please don't underestimate their intelligence. Hey, they started a business of their own, which means they've got the sense, so you have to make sure to step to them with respect and total honesty, you'll have a much better chance.

Just as you did with the investors, you need to figure out all of your expenses. Artist fees, flights, hotels, food, promotions, ground transportation etc. Break these expenses down to the dime and then sort them in order of importance. This task alone will be difficult as you will realize that they're all important. No sense in raising money for flights when you haven't yet booked anyone to fly. So instead, try sorting according to price which would of course put the artist at the top of the list. Now remember, you don't have to pay the artist's fee all at once, fifty percent is all you need to secure the act, and you might be able to do that with your own funds and still raise more to pay off the balance, on the day of the show.

Now when deciding on what to ask, and from who, let's take a look at what we need, because there might be other ways of dealing with this, for example, we need ground transportation for the artists, and depending on what kind of vehicle we're getting, and whether or not it comes with a driver, will determine its cost, but hold up! Why would we need money for this?

The transportation company, whether it's a rental, and we get Uncle Paul to drive, or a professionally Chauffeured limousine, is a perfect prospect to approach for sponsorship, but not for money, but rather the service! In return we can place their logo on our promotional material, shout outs on our Social Medias, and a sincere thank you along with a plug from the stage the night of the show.

We can give them a few tickets to give to either their staff or their customers, or what about a VIP table for the bosses?

This type of deal can work with others such as restaurants and hotels. Make a list of all of the potential sponsors whose services would work just as good as money. Keep this list handy and keep building it.

As for competing businesses, this is when your integrity has to stand tall. If Tommy's Clothing Store already agreed to sponsor, please don't go across the street and ask David's Clothing store too. You're just looking for trouble and next time, neither will work with you, however in the beginning, do solicit both, but only go with one. Which one? No, not the one who offered the most, but rather the one who you can see yourself do business with for years to come.

So in closing this topic, remember, Sponsors are great sources for funding, and the true beauty of it all is, you don't have to pay them back!

SIMPLE STEP #3

CHOOSING THE CLUB

Hassan Martinez: *I look for an upscale venue that is unique, clean and gives me a very fair door and bar deal and most of all, someone I can build a relationship with. Definitely has to cater to the crowd I'm targeting at the time which is mostly 30 plus, although recently my audience has been a lot younger than 30 now (mommas bringing their daughter's).... these days I have been doing 500 to 1000 capacity only because we are selling out in advance and have created a series for longevity.*

I always say, it's best to start with a smaller place that you can sell out, than a larger place that might look empty. Energy is everything when you have an event. The acts feed off of the crowd and the crowd feeds off of the acts. People come to an event to have a good time, in a safe environment, so work that into your Mission Statement! This book as you already know focuses on Freestyle events for the Night Club, but it might be of some use to get an idea as to the capacities of various venues, because a successful run of events might have you thinking about an upscale. Note: these numbers are not etched in stone, as capacities may vary beyond these numbers, but through my own experience, these are the capacities I personally would assign to each.

1. Bars and Pubs under 100 People capacity
2. Lounges less than 300 people capacity
3. Banquet Halls 500 to 800
4. *Night clubs less than 1500*
5. Theaters 1500 plus
6. Amphitheaters 3000 plus
7. Outdoor Festivals up to 10,000
8. Arenas 10,000 plus
9. Stadiums 20,000 plus

I'm sure there are others that I might be overlooking, but these should give you an idea as to what might be out there, and choosing the right venue with the right capacity for your event can be the deciding factor between success and failure.

Of course what your budget will be will determine on the size of the club. If it's too small, you might have to charge too much at the door, and if it's too big, a decent turn out might still make the place look empty and unsuccessful.

One of the best ways of trying to figure out what to charge for your tickets would be to simply see what similar events charged there in the past.

Charlie Rodriguez: Location, Location, Location. Easy Access to the nearest highway. No one wants to drive on a local street at 2:00 am after drinking. You need a minimum space to accommodate your biggest show. Popularity of the club doesn't really matter. The people are following the promoter's name. The club isn't so important.

One of the first questions I ask a promoter when they call me is, what kind of venue are you talking about? And after they tell me, I find out that the reason they decided on that particular venue was usually because it was available, whether for free or at a discount.

Deals like this have to be thoroughly thought out because venues don't just give up their space. It cost them money just to open the doors. Understanding this will be crucial to the deal you end up with, and even if the owner gives you a night for free, he still might insist on some sort of bar guarantee. So let's talk quickly about the Bar Guarantee, and more or less how it works.

JI Starr: In the beginning there were many times that I didn't even pay my own bills, to make sure I had enough to cover the bar guarantee, just in case my night was a flop.

Bar Guarantees

When you own a club, the bar is where the "real" money is made, so it makes sense for them to give up the door to a promoter, because for every ten dollars the promoter might make at the door, the owner can make anywhere from fifty to a hundred at the bar. In the beginning you're not going to have too much leverage. The ball will be in the club's court, even if the night you are after is a dead one, but it is still an opportunity, and if you can prove to them that you can make things happen, the owner may possibly work out a better deal later on. Bar guarantees are usually calculated by the owner according to what it would cost him or her to open the doors and bring in staff. Some owners might want this guarantee up front, others might be willing to take it from the door, it depends on the individual and how they like doing business. I've seen promoters put up anywhere from $300 to $3,000 in bar guarantee, depending on the size of the club as well as the amount of people it took to run the night.

Nick Minsky: In Chicago location is everything. If you're going to be a successful promoter, the Club must have a 4:00 AM license.

In the beginning you can pretty much expect a bar guarantee. The owner doesn't know you, and you have no experience. But prove to him that you can pull it off, and he might just sweeten the deal, so be patient. Clubs get the bulk of their business on the weekends, mostly Saturdays, with Fridays right behind, and Sunday's according to whether or not

Monday's a holiday.

Thursdays can sometimes work, but usually when they're promoted as "After Work" parties, with discounted drinks and a free buffet. Those nights usually end early, and having acts perform isn't the norm, and I myself wouldn't recommend it.

What Club Owners Look For in a Promoter

Some of you who are reading this book, have never promoted before, which means the number one question that you will be asked will indeed hit a brick wall. *"So what experience do you have?"* Preparing yourself for this one question will lay the tracks needed to land this club. Right off the bat, I have to say it, please don't lie! Club owners are businesspeople, and whether you ever want to agree or not, trust me, they're not dumb!

James Rios: Choosing a venue is imperative to a successful event! When looking for a venue you must first and foremost look at the demographic of the location. Putting on an event in an area that isn't known for the type of talent you are trying to bring is the first sign of failure. Then you have to consider Size of the Venue and history for hosting events. Parking availability, capacity, and sound ordinances if any. Other things to consider such as if late hours permitted? Is there ample room for the artist to perform with an adequate distance between them and the crowd, and last but not least how will the added sound and live vocals affect the acoustics? Most won't think about this until they experience a night of ear shattering feedback.

Club owners are not too concerned about how great of a party you can throw, but rather how many people you can pull in, and how many of them will be drinking. So keep that in mind when speaking with owners.

Approaching The Owner

Go to the club on different nights to get a better idea of how they pull and when. If it's a Friday, and the club is open and staffed, but there are only a few people at the bar, that club is clearly struggling. And though it's a bad situation for them, for you it's an opportunity, so don't blow it!

Plan, not just your strategy, but more importantly, your approach! Because approaching an owner at the wrong time could easily ruin any opportunity you might've had. The best time to approach club owners are early weekdays, when the club is open, but dead.

This is the day you catch the owner taking inventory of the bar, fixing something that is too small to hire someone else to do, or maybe just sitting at the bar having himself a drink, in deep thought about why the hell did he ever open a club. Well, this is the time you need to get with him, but hold up, not so fast, it's not going to be that easy. Number one, you are still inexperienced, and number two, this guy has no idea of who the hell you are! Now mind you, there are plenty of first time promoters who are going to have it a little easier. They either know the owner, someone who knows the owner, or maybe already work for him, and God bless them, but what I'm going to address here is the other ninety-eight percent of the first time promoters, who don't know anyone.

So, you figure out that *one* day that the doors are open, music is blaring but the place is empty, and you stop in for a drink, and if you don't drink, I still recommend you order one. You're not going to get much attention from a promoter, sitting their sipping on a Coke, besides, that would seem too suspicious. Now don't go getting smashed, that's not going to help either. All you want to do is somehow make contact with the owner. Let him see you, so that the next time you come back, which should be the following week, he remembers you.

Chuck Lamagra: *Location, size, popularity, not to mention a Great Deal should all play a role in choosing the right club, because these days if the entire formula isn't there, the event can suffer.*

Make contact again, and this time, greet him with a simple hello. Please don't stare at this guy, or even force a conversation, just let it flow comfortably and before you know it, he'll recognize you each and every time, and soon you'll no longer be a stranger.

I know this process may seem a bit tedious and drawn out, but remember what you are doing, you need a spot to promote, and even though your intentions are to help him and his business, trust me when I say, he's already been approached, many times.

In the best case scenario, the owner might actually pull up a stool beside you and start a conversation himself, and at that moment you have just gained the best seat in the house, so don't blow it!

In this seat you are to basically listen and observe. Introduce yourself, and don't linger. Be prepared for the conversation between you and the owner. Things such as what you do for a living, have you ever been to this club on a good night, or why do you come here every Thursday at 6:00 pm, have one drink and then leave? Have some answers prepared, and one day, when you're his top promoter, you can reveal your strategy, I'm sure he'll get a kick out of it.

So a couple of months have passed, you've shown up on that off night at least eight times, and you and the owner are on a friendly first name basis, he's probably even bought you a couple of drinks by now. By this time you should also have quite a bit of information about him and his club, such as how long he's had it, is this his first? And are there any regrets. You should also be familiar with the troubles he is having and which nights can really use a boost, and BAM!!!... That's it, your cue!

But what should you say? Well, during those two months that you're working the owner, you should also be working your approach. By this time you would be very comfortable speaking with him, you guys are no longer strangers, and you understand his situation which makes you the best candidate it to help fix it. Doing it this way may even help you establish a deal that is more beneficial than had you just come off the street and ask for a spot.

You could end up not being required to pay any bar guarantees, or even rent. It can be so good that the owner might consider giving you a small piece of the bar revenue, or possibly offer to finance your idea, which would then have you totally skipping over Simple Step #2.

The keys here are patience and observation, and with a sincere intention of trying to help the owner solve one of his biggest problems, will eventually place you in the position of one of his club promoters.

Luis Pinto: *Location is a no brainer, that's very important, although I find you have a better chance of being successful if the club is willing to invest in your night. Back in the day clubs would give you just a percentage of the door, now I go into a deal with intentions of getting a percentage of the door and the bar, and if they have radio time to include my night, I try to get that too.*

SIMPLE STEP #4

CHOOSING THE RIGHT ARTIST

Chuck Lamagra: *We normally do polls via our Social Networks to try and figure out what artists the people would like to see. Once that's figured out and the artist is booked, we promote the hell out of it. By the way, the first artist I ever booked was Kenny Rogers. Lol*

Artists are a part of your team, and unhappy artists like unhappy employees' makes for an unhappy customer. Understanding the Artists will place you on a whole other level as there are promoters out there who do not find this to be important, or even necessary. So many times I've gotten calls from would be promoters asking me about the Artists. They heard that they're pretty affordable and can draw a great crowd, yet they don't know who the Artists are or what they sing. In fact, I run across so many promoters who are just totally unfamiliar with anything Freestyle, some actually going so far as to brag about their successful dealings outside of the genre, such as Hip Hop, Latin or Pop genres. As if to say that Freestyle is so below what they are used to doing, so therefore, this should be a cinch. But come on now, if you really were as successful as you say, why would you even entertain the thought of dabbling elsewhere?

Hassan Martinez: I would advise to start off small and build. You are building a fan base and longevity. I've seen a lot of promoters come and go because they went too big, too fast.

Unfortunately, there are so many Booking Agents who don't even care, so long as they book the show, because that's the only way they'll get paid. But what good is a promoter to any of us if he or she keeps taking hits. A promoter's success is vital to the success of the agent, and without either of us, the artists might as well hang up their mics.

You don't have to be an expert to be a fan. You only have to enjoy the music. You don't always have to know all the hits, who sang them, who produced them and what label they were released. Your only obligation as a fan is to listen, enjoy and hopefully buy! But as a *Promoter?* Now that's a different story because understanding your Artists is like a Pharmacist understanding his medicines. All medicines do not heal all ailments. In fact, prescribing the wrong medicine can actually be fatal.

People who are subjected to certain regions sometimes have no idea just how vast the Freestyle genre is. That practically every corner of the U.S. as well as abroad have their own favorites when it comes to Freestyle. Some of their favorites are actually from their region, others are not. Knowing this is very important as there are headlining artists from New York, who couldn't pack an elevator in California, and vice versa.

Charlie Rodriguez: Bust out with the biggest artist you can find and make a statement! I did my first show and had 10,000 people in attendance with no experience. There is no time to play games, give it your best shot right from the gate. The artists I book are determined by the music that is playing on rotation on your local radio station.

I'm all for breaking artists into new areas, but there's a time, place, and absolute way of doing that, and placing that type of responsibility on a new promoter, or at least one new to the genre, can be catastrophic for us all.

Many times when speaking with a new promoter about a possible booking, they sometimes inquire about artists who I know for sure cannot draw in their particular area. So what is it? Is it that they themselves are fans? That's cool, buy their music! But don't book them for a show, at least not now!

What sells Freestyle events these days more than ever are the "Names." That's right, names sell! And nobody understands this better than Phony Freestyle acts, but we'll get to that a little later!

Except for the fanatical, typical fans of the music, can't

always connect the dots between faces, songs, and names. Many times you've loved a song and never knew who sang it, or knew about an artist but couldn't name any of their songs, so as a promoter it is vital that you make these connections, because you could be missing out on a whole lot of audience.

New promoters can easily be influenced, whether it be by the club owner, a relative, or even a fan or two. However, it's important to be able to decipher whether that influence is based on business, or fanaticism. Just because someone is a fan of a particular artist, doesn't mean that they would work out in your particular club.

The promoter's own personal research is invaluable, and nowadays, with the Internet there are no excuses. Your research can be as intensive as it needs to be, right from the comforts of your own home, and between that and the suggestions provided by your trusty booking agent, you should be set and ready to go. However, if you are still not one hundred percent sure about your choice, then it might be worth it to try and somehow reach out to someone from whichever radio station in your area that might still be playing, or at least use to play Freestyle. Many stations have Old School mix shows that can really help you out, and just by listening in will help confirm your choice. Trust me when I tell you, the station already did their homework. They tested the market, and if you're looking for suggestions, you really can't get any better than a radio station.

James Rios: The first thing I would tell you is to start off small, with an artist who you believe will draw a crowd but understand that if you are a new promoter, people may be weary so I would suggest trying to at least break on your first show with whatever artist you bring. More importantly than the money you would have established a reputation for the quality of the show. Once you have done that, you can pick and choose your artist by what you think will work. Now with all that being said, go see the artist perform and ask questions about them, their professionalism, and quite frankly their ego!! (Do they feel that they're better than the people who come to see them?) I would rather bring someone who is humble, appreciative, with a little less draw, than an egotistical, arrogant prick! Remember they can make or break the reputation that you have worked so hard to build.

I've had new promoters send me their wish list, only to find a bunch of artists who, even with the most seasoned promoters would be a difficult sell. My next question is always, so how'd you come up with this list? And just as I thought, these were recommendations from people who do not belong recommending anything, or even worst, recommendations from within that particular artist's camp, or even the artists themselves. But what happens if the event ends up being dead. Only twelve people show up. The promoter was relying on the door to cover the balance, and now doesn't have it. The show is canceled, and the next day all negativity breaks out on Social Media. This isn't good for any of us, whether we were involved in that particular event or not, and now another Freestyle promoter bites the dust.

Every Freestyle event represents every Artist, Promoter, Manager, and Agent. It happens all the time, where after a successful event, my phone starts ringing off the hook, with promoters who had heard about the success of a particular event and now want to book the same if not a similar line up in hopes that *that* was the magic key. But it wasn't, all it was, was the result of intense research, hard work, and a passion to take it to the end.

Oh, and don't forget to always try and consult with your friendly neighborhood booking agent, if anyone has an incentive to see you win, it's them!

What's In A Name

The most valuable asset an artist has is his or her name! People can be huge fans of the music, and not necessarily know the name of the act who recorded it. But those who frequent club and concert events or others, are very familiar with the name, as it is the name that draws the crowd, or better yet, it is the name that sells tickets!

In fact I am currently working a multiple act concert, and as I present various acts as potential features, the promoter keeps asking me this one question. How many tickets do you think that artist can sell? An extremely difficult question, if not impossible as I've experienced firsthand so many scenarios. From A-Listers with poor turn outs, to B-Listers with Sold Out events. I am a firm believer that a successful event does not rely on just one aspect of the deal. It is without doubt a collaborative effort, with an emphasis on the promoter. In other words, I feel that a weak artist with a strong promoter has a better chance of success, than a strong artist with a weak promoter.

JI Starr: I've always booked artists that were currently on the radio. Of course i would have a relatively unknown open so that the flyer would look busy. If the venue was a large one, then a major act can get you an amazing ROI. But if it was a small venue I would of course hire a smaller act that was still somehow relevant, and keep the admission to a minimum to make sure that I packed the room.

You see, technically, the artist already did their job, by recording the hits. The fans are there, and use of the artist's name is necessary to attract their attention. However, attracting their attention doesn't always guarantee ticket sales. That is the job of the promoter... To Promote!

The name is what the artists allow the promoters to use to do their job, because without it, promoting can be quite difficult, if not altogether impossible.

Artist Fees

Negotiating Artist's Fees... Hmm, does it really exist? Can you truly negotiate an artist out of their typical asking fee? It depends on how you look at it. I as an agent know through experience how low an artist has gone in the past, as well as how high. I don't always agree on what some artists might charge, and just as some might charge too high, some I feel charge too little.

But it is the artist's choice as to what they want to charge, just as it is the promoter's choice as to what they are willing to spend. So most of the time, when it comes to artist's price, I tend to stand back a bit, and try and observe the deal from a distance.

If the promoter is new to the game, his club is small, and the budget's tight, yet he's got his eye set on a particular artist, depending on whether or not I have experience booking that act at a lower price in the past, I have no problem approaching that artist with an offer, because sometimes, for some artist, it isn't worth losing a gig for just a few hundred dollars.

But the bottom line is this. If an artist is willing to totally lose a show because the fee isn't what they are asking, and the promoter just doesn't have the budget to offer more, then both sides must be respected, and it is then up to me to go back to the roster and find someone else that could possibly fit the deal.

Nick Huminski: Generally you choose an Artist based on what your clientele base likes. You survey your following to see what the majority likes. Never take a chance on a wild card Artist, because you will most likely take a loss and that will be the end of your promoting career, unless of course you have deep pockets and can afford the loss.

There are some ways however to get even the most stubborn artist down a bit, and this technique works in practically any business. Offer them multiple shows. Sounds easy, doesn't it? Well, it's not! And this is why. For an artist to show any interest in lowering their price for multiple shows, their first requirement is going to be that those shows run back to back, and that all deposits are made at or around the same time. Want to get a good deal on an artist? Book them for a Thursday, Friday, and Saturday, and you can save quite a bit of money, and the artist will be ecstatic! But there's more to it than that. The shows will have to be close to one another, preferable driving distance. If you're sending an artist on a three day run from New York to Los Angeles, then to Miami, there's a good chance that the price won't change much if at all, or the artists might pass on one or two of them.

So what would work? A short three day Tri-State tour, that's what! Say Friday, Saturday, Sunday in New York, New Jersey, and Connecticut. How about San Jose, San Francisco and Modesto? You get the idea. The trick though is making sure that you are not violating any radius clauses. For instance, some of my contracts might state that another show cannot be booked 90 days prior and within a 75 mile radius of any other shows they might be on. Challenging but not impossible, and with some thought and a little innovation this could really work in your favor. The only other way something like this can work where the radius wouldn't matter is if all the shows are booked by the same promoter. Either that or all the promoters are in agreement. These deals can be quite tricky. Sometimes they run smooth, other times they could be a complete nightmare, so be careful!

Say No To Phonies

James Rios: When it comes to dealing with Phonies, just think about your reputation, and ask yourself this, Do you really want to be known as the promoter who will bring anyone just to make a buck, or are you yourself a true fan and believer in that those who created the music, should be the ones who perform it?

Here's a subject I'm sure many wondered whether or not I'd even bring up, and of course I would!
I personally have been fighting Phonyism within the Freestyle genre for well over fifteen years, and though it sprung from the scandal surrounding The Cover Girls, I realized that they weren't the only victims, and therefore made it my mission to put an end to Phonyism within the Freestyle genre once and for all.

Nick Huminski: Not many promoters know the History or the politics behind certain Artist's, and rely solely on the recommendations given them by their booking agent. This can be a problem as agents have also been known to mislead, therefore it is extremely important for Promoters to do their own homework, and make sure that when they book an artist, that it's the "Real" artist!

I am a huge fan of both cover bands and tribute artists. I feel that they play a vital role in the preservation of music in general. They allow those who haven't, or never will have the opportunity to experience an original act live, get a bit of a glimpse into what it might be like. As long as it is clear, and unquestionable that these artists are paying tribute, I support it wholeheartedly. But then there are Phonies! Those acts who have blatantly hi-jacked the identities of our original artists, whether through legal loopholes, and misinformation, take advantage of the ignorant and misinformed. I plead with all the new promoters to please, DO NOT participate in this despicable act. Help us maintain the integrity of at least, the Freestyle genre as I feel that it is one of the ones most violated. Help protect it, so that future generations can honor and enjoy the works of our Legendary Freestyle Artists!

JI Starr: well I never understood why certain acts would have different members. I always felt that they should use a different name. I've run across this problem with Pajama Party, Sweet Sensation, Exposé, Giggles and later with the Cover Girls, and TKA.

I find Freestyle promoters to be some of the smartest people in this business. To be able to repackage and successfully sell events that were first introduced to the public decades ago is an incredible feat. However, the moment I catch a promoter, participating somehow, someway in Phonyism, is the moment that I lose all respect, and that admiration I once had, goes flying out the window. Any promoter who says that they did not realize that they were booking Phonies, have not only become the biggest dummies I know, but now also the biggest liars, and they need to immediately remove themselves from the business!

Chuck Lamagra: *The fighting between Artists and Phony Acts, has without doubt hurt the genre. Tickets don't sell like they use to as nowadays, fans are never sure as to who might actually be performing at an event!*

SIMPLE STEP #5

PROMOTING YOUR EVENT

Chuck Lamagra: On-line Dating Sites have been my #1 best and most cost effective way of getting the word out about my shows.

Marketing can exist without Promotions, but Promotions cannot exist without Marketing, make sense? Okay, let me try and explain it this way. You see, Marketing is the File Cabinet, and Promotions is just one of the files inside. All together there are four files. The other three are the product or service you are providing, in the case of Club Promotions, you are offering the service of Entertainment. The next two files would be the Price, a huge factor that many decide by just pulling a number out of the air, and the place or location from which you will be entertaining. In the real estate game it's all about location location location, and with any business that requires human traffic, location is still king. Don't believe me? Then try and promote a club in an area where cars are known to be broken into, or where the neighbors are always complaining about the loud music. This list can go on.

These four files within that file cabinet are called the 4 P's of marketing, Product, Price, Place, and Promotion. So now you understand what I mean when I say that Marketing can exist without promotions, but not the other way around. So let's skip those other files for now as we do touch on them throughout this book, and let us dive right into Promotions.

There are many ways to promote your event, and in this age we are so fortunate to have the Internet as it is filled with great ideas, techniques and tools to help us do things that we could never have done back in the day, and as much as I would love to get into the fine details of this incredible subject, I must pull back a bit and present to you the absolute simplest. I want to assume that you are working with little to no money as my goal is to get you up and running as soon as possible, because from there you'll be able to take your venture to whatever heights you desire.

The idea of promotions in its purest form is to communicate with your potential audience. Mind you now that I did not say *an* Audience, or *every* audience, or even *any* audience, I specified *Your Potential Audience!* And if you haven't figured out who that is according to your location, then you must rewind and start over, because you can't sell something without knowing who would buy it.

So right off the bat you are probably saying to yourself, well, my audience are Freestyle lovers. Okay, great, and how do you figure that? Are they all wearing I Love Freestyle Tee shirts? Or maybe there's a secret hand sign that they flash so that you recognize who they are? No, it's none of that. Freestyle lovers have a sort community, just like Hip Hop, Rock, Gospel and so on. Many of them have a lot in common, starting with where they live, because one thing that many friends have in common is the music they like. Think about your closest friends and you will see that most of them pretty much like the same kind of music you do.

If Freestyle events are known to have come to your area in the past and done reasonably well, then there is a good chance that a significant Freestyle community might still exist there. But what if they're not? What if you've never heard of any Freestyle event happening in the area, does that mean there are no fans there? Not at all! So how would you go about finding these Freestyle fans that you would need to pull off a successful event?

Nick Huminski: *Have a very strong work ethic. If you have to work 24 hours a day 7 days a week to meet your goal, then do it. Hard work and perseverance pays off in the end!*

After you've secured your night, make sure it's going to be a regular thing because it is going to take time to build. Start out with just a night of Freestyle music. Find a DJ that knows the music, and of course has enough to cover the night. DJ's are always on the lookout for some type of residency, and the smart ones will do whatever it takes to get that, even if that means playing for little to no money, at least at the beginning.

If the club already has a DJ, that's even better, but if that DJ doesn't fit the bill, he might have to be switched up for another, and there's a good chance that the owner might even help you out with that.

Pick a name for your event and make sure to include the word Freestyle in it, it's a keyword and is an absolute must. Events such as Freestyle Explosion, Freestyle Festival, and Freestyle Extravaganza which are some of the best examples should be enough to prove what I am saying. Just come up with something catchy, and easy to remember, and of course, unique, as trying to use the name of an already established event can cause problems for everyone. This event name is going to become the brand. Hence the word *Brand* which is what farmers do to their livestock with a branding iron. This is what you are trying to do as well, is brand the name of your event into the minds of your potential audience. But please, I don't mean it literally, so I better not read about it in the paper!

So you start off with say, Freestyle Fridays, which I don't really consider an event brand, but rather more of a tag, and as long as you are the only Freestyle Fridays in your market, then they could work until you establish a decent following. Your doors open from 8:00pm till 2:00am. That's six hours, or lets say 360 minutes, divide that by approximate three minute song, and you are looking at about 120 Freestyle songs to be played without repeating. Is that possible? Oh, absolutely! There is so much Freestyle music out there, both the classics as well as new stuff that running out of music will be your least worry.

So the night could sound a little boring. Non-stop Freestyle music playing. Some people dancing, others just sitting around and talking, and practically everyone drinking. But that shouldn't be it. This is now your opportunity to work the floor. Make your rounds, meet the people, thank'em for coming, and tell them to bring their friends. You have a huge job here because this is going to play an important role in establishing yourself as a promoter.

Get up on the stage, give some Happy Birthday shout outs. Acknowledge your DJ, and thank your owner. Even if there's only five people in your crowd, this is your time to build, don't hide because the turn out wasn't what you expected, go out there and make sure that next week, those same five come back, and this time bring their friends.

How about some Freestyle Trivia? Where whoever answers correctly gets two free admissions for the following week, a free drink ticket, tee shirt, hat, or even a key chain. Doesn't matter, people love free shit! I know I do.

If you can build a solid audience without any performances, just imagine what you can do when you finally start featuring acts. Again, the key here is patience and observation. Do not take this very important time for granted. Don't just sit around with your friends drinking and showing off. Go to work!

So how do you actually get people in the door? Do you just open, and they come? We wish, but nope, it's going to require a little more than that. Some work, some money, and a whole lot of creativity!

Social media is a Godsend to the promoter. No more standing on the corner at 2:00 am in minus degree weather to hand out flyers that you paid a fortune for. Now you can sit at home, in your pajamas and be just as productive as ever, so long as you keep in mind that, so can your competitors!

So what can you do to stand out? Spamming other people's pages can be a real turn off, and that's the last thing any promoter wants to be. So depending on which Social Medias are popular, use them to attract the people. Whether it be with hot topics, pretty girls, great advice, or humor, just get them on-board, and mixed in with all the other entertaining stuff, and then... Post your flyer! You don't want to bang people over the head with it, they'll sense when you're doing that, and quickly change the channel. Instead, like a hot apple pie, place it on the window sill and let the aroma go to work.

Back in the day, Promoters used what was called street teams. Every promoter bragged about their street team, and understood their value. They would spend three hundred dollars for five thousand flyers, and then pay three kids a hundred dollars each to distribute flyers outside clubs. The task was no joke, and promoters only hoped that their street team was reliable.

On-line ticket sales didn't exist back in the day, so there was no way of predicting the success of an up-coming event the way you can now. In fact, the only time you were able to realize the success an event was at the end of the night when you were cashing out.

So study the Internet, particularly what's going on through Social Media, who's doing what, where, and most importantly... how!

JI Starr: Radio coop advertising with the major beverage companies, use to save me some money, as well as having them sponsor the cost of the flyer and in turn I would become the presenting sponsor. Over the years, these types of promotions have changed drastically.

Flyers

Promoting on Social Media would make no sense if we didn't have something visual to present. Just a bunch of words on a post just won't cut it. Probably the most basic yet viable form of promotions still in existence today is none other than the good ol' promotional flyer. That 4X6 inch postcard that you find advertising club and concert events. As mentioned above, these things were usually printed at about five thousand at a time, and people were hired to stand outside clubs and pass them out.

For some promoters this was their only means of promoting their events, and unlike today where computers can handle practically the entire process, the promotional flyer and its distribution took as much thought and planning as the event itself.

The process usually began with a meeting with the printer. You would either try and explain to them what you wanted, or if possible, sketch out the idea on a sheet of paper. Finding the right fonts, images, and colors, and then arranging them in various layouts took a lot of thought as once you approved it, there was no going back, at least not without being charged extra.

The computer term we use today called Cut & Paste was something that was done... literally. Printers would cut out letters and images and paste different arrangements onto a sheet of paper. Not only was this process intricate and time consuming, it was also quite expensive, and once the arrangement was approved, a master plate was made which was then used to print the actual copies.

Over the years the promotional flyer has maintained its popularity, while becoming easier to design and distribute thanks to the many programs and Social sites available.

Teaching you how to create the perfect flyer can send this book into a whole other realm, and since there is so much information about this on-line, I would rather just advise you to search; *How to produce an effective flyer,* and make sure you have a pen and pad ready because trust me, there is a lot of information available, but if you just wanna get the ball rolling without having to read anymore, here's a quick tip that you can use immediately.

Don't try and reinvent the flyer, just use the ol' tried and true, Copy Cat technique, a technique that's been used in business since the beginning of time. The process is simple. Find a flyer that you absolutely love, and try and recreate it as best as you can, changing of course the information. Do this a few times and you will eventually find yourself combining the best of many, therefore creating something that you can honestly call, your own.

James Rios: One of the keys to every event that I have done that has been a huge success is finding the right people to get involved. Once you establish your team, research what works with the genre of music you are bringing in and utilize it. In my opinion, Radio is Dead, Flyers is right behind it. I use 100% social media to promote all my events now.

Social Media

How did we ever live without it? These days we find old friends, stay in touch with relatives, and meet new people on a daily basis. But Social Media has also another important purpose, and that is promoting businesses. Well, why shouldn't it? It's an incredible medium and anyone who refuses to use it for their promotional benefits are going to have a tough time trying to compete.

As of this writing, sites such as Facebook, Twitter, and YouTube are king, and in years to come I'm sure many others will either join them, or even take their place.

Study these sites, and how organizations put them to work promoting their businesses. No more standing on corners passing out flyers, begging magazines and newspapers for some publicity, or even dishing out major cash for a few measly seconds of radio and television time. Instead put that money into figuring out new ways of using the Internet to market your business. Keep in mind that it also made it easer for everyone, and that includes your competitors. So the key here is not to just do it, but rather to do it better, and faster than anyone else.

Word Of Mouth

Hassan Martinez: I have always been personable which helped me build tons of relationships throughout the years.

Today, Social Media and Word Of Mouth go hand in hand. In fact, Social Media has taken word of mouth to a whole other level. Have you ever watched a movie that just blew you away, to the point that as you left the theater, you caught yourself telling others as they walked in what a great movie it was? Then you get home, and tell family and friends the same thing? This is called word of mouth marketing, and it is the most effective of all marketing for one simple reason... People believe it!

Advertisements on the other hand are paid campaigns developed by those who have a direct incentive for the movie to do well. They produce these incredible movie trailers that highlight the best parts. They run ads in every major newspaper, and they get reviews from critics whose job it is to give reviews. This process when done right is very effective. However, it is also very expensive!

People rush the theaters for this incredible experience that they've been subliminally force-fed, only to leave the theater terribly disappointed. But by then, box office records have already been broken, which then sends the campaign into a sort of organic whirlwind of promotions, and will continue until the cycle eventually burns itself out, and by then the companies have made a substantial amount of money.

As for your Freestyle event, especially if it's your first one, you can release on-line promos that will excite the people to the point that they start talking about it, because that is when significant sales will take place, and once you get them into the club, continue doing things that will have them not only anticipating your next event, but also enticing others to come along.

Charlie Rodriguez: You make a name by sticking to your game plan and not changing it. Long term branding is the key. There is no short cut to long term sustainability. You have to put the time in. Do not change your product. This is the Kiss Of Death!

Branding

Your brand should not only sell the event at hand, but if done properly, should sell every event from there on. I've personally experienced two types of branding when it came to Freestyle promoters. Those that brand themselves or their companies, and those who brand a theme. For example, a promoter that brands his or herself might use a name such as *John Doe Presents*, while a promoter who brands a theme might call all of their events something like *The Freestyle Concert Series.*

Neither way is wrong, and I've seen both reach incredible success, however, much thought must be made in how you want to brand it because it will have a definite effect on future promotions.

A promoter, who uses the theme of their event as the brand, is what I would consider a *Hard Seller*, meaning they're clear and concise as to what it is they are selling, and their audience is specific. These types of themes usually always use the word Freestyle in their branding. Obviously, the downfall to this technique is the fact that after putting so much time, energy, and possibly money into this type of branding, to suddenly want to switch genres, or possibly promote something UN-Freestyle related, would mean having to start over, because the brand then would make no sense. However, a promoter who uses *their* name or company, without any reference to the word Freestyle, though they have the freedom to explore other types of events, as their brand does not subject them to just one type. The downfall to this technique is that it is NOT a Hard sell, therefore it takes much more time, energy and money to connect the dots between your name, and the market you are after. People will not immediately know what it is you are selling unless they read deeper, which would be your task at hand.

Whichever way you decide to go is totally up to you, and how you can determine which one to go with is to decide whether you feel that Freestyle is all you ever want to do, or do you think in the future you might want to explore other areas.

Theme branding of course would be the fastest and easiest route to go as it leaves no question as to who your audience is, and what they are buying. However you will be pigeonholed into an area whereas if you ever decide to switch, you will most like have to hit the restart button, and after investing so much time, money and energy into your brand, it would really suck to have to abandon it.

Other than that, there is really no right or wrong way to do this, nor is one better than the other. It's all based on your individual goal, so give it enough thought and once you decide, give it all you have!

SIMPLE STEP #6

SHOWTIME

JI Starr: Always check your equipment, because in reality most of the time its not yours and you don't know the maintenance schedule if any that it gets.

So it's the day of the show, what do we do? Well everything we've done up to now was to prepare us for this day, which means this day should be perfect. The goal of this day is that it runs as smooth as it possibly can. All problems have already been dealt with, snags fixed, and miscommunications clarified. Your attention from here on should be to make sure the show goes well. If you're still trying to get people to come, then your focus will be off, and you will be jeopardizing those who had come for those who haven't. If you are still insistent on promoting up to the last minute, then I would advise you to get someone else to do it. Your attention needs to be on the show. Is the DJ all set? Do you need any other equipment? If you haven't yet paid the artist, do you have the cash balance ready and available? Is there communication between the artist and the driver? Have you briefed your security, and possibly done a walk-through of how, and by whom would the artist be escorted. Do you know where you will be holding the meet and greet? Are there tables and chairs ready? Do you have a waitress on standby to service the artist, and is everything requested on the rider good to go?

So as you can see, there is still a lot of work to be done, and this work is the part that will be acknowledged by the artist, more so than even the turn out. So on the day of the show, focus on just that, making sure the day runs smooth.

The Track Show

One of the great benefits of starting out your promotions career with Freestyle is due to the fact that as of right now, all Freestyle acts usually perform to track. What does that mean? Well, it means they require no technical back line. No band, no equipment rentals, nothing. Just a track that plays either through the venue's permanent in-house system or one that is set up specifically for your event.

The medium to which the artists store this track has evolved throughout the years. From old quarter inch reels, which were a hassle to travel with, and extremely delicate, to Digital Audio Tapes (DATS), Compact Disc (CDs) and currently MP3s stored on thumb drives, and copied to the DJ's computer for playback. Now how does this benefit you as a promoter? Well, track shows are the most inexpensive means for a live performance. This has become a standard in Freestyle and therefore it is expected and totally accepted by the fans.

In regards to track shows, I've learned a few things over the years. One of the most important being that the Freestyle fans want to hear the songs as they've always heard them. Which means, artists who tend to perform to remixed versions of their hits, usually receive a much weaker response than those who perform to the original. The TV track was the preferred version at one time, as it was produced especially for live performances. But over the years many of these TV tracks were no longer available, not to mention, some of the venues had equipment that was less than acceptable, and a track that relied totally on the artist's vocals was sometimes compromised, so as years went on, I found myself using the Radio Mix version more than anything. Radio Mixes are those that were produced specifically for radio. Many singles, especially in Freestyle were known to be released with a bunch of mixes, such as the Club Mix, the Dub Mix, The House Mix etc... But from all of those mixes, the most important mix was of course,

The Radio Mix. It is the mix produced with the hope of reaching the most people. The Radio Mix requires a specific formula, dictated by the radio industry to make songs more suitable for airplay. These formulas include such things as, shortened intros and outros, edited hook lines, and instrumental breaks totally cut out. The lengths of these mixes are kept to just about three minutes.

Track shows, depending on how many hits the artists have, range in length from about twelve to thirty minutes, with the average stopping at around twenty. These lengths have nothing to do with what you pay for. It's been determined by each individual artist according to years of experiment. These are the lengths that work for them, and not always do these lengths determine how many songs are performed. That determination relies on how their show tapes have been pieced together.

I've seen thirty minute shows with just four songs, and twenty minute shows with as many as nine. So be sure to ask that question. "How long is the show?" and, "How many songs do they perform?" What I wouldn't do though, is try and suggest, or customize a show. Not only would it probably not work, it is also outright insulting to the artist. So please, book it for what it is, and if the show seems too short, or too long, work with it, and trust that the artists know what they're doing.

Another great benefit to the track show is that it can be accommodated just about anywhere. Many of the more established Freestyle acts today have been doing this for quite some time, and though these days they may be a bit more picky as to where they perform, back when it all started, there were no boundaries.

From pubs to parks, restaurants to arenas, if they were paying we were playing, and enjoyed every minute of it. Besides the type of establishment we performed, another challenge we faced was the set up. Flipped over speakers with the big hole in the middle, to pool tables, and steps, dubbed as stages, but we pulled it off and still put on great shows. Without us even realizing it, these situations built character, and created a level of intimacy unparalleled to any other genre of music. It's no wonder our music still exist! A big topic that has come up with Freestyle artists and their track shows is the misconception about Lip-Syncing! For as many years as I've worked behind the scenes of this business, I myself have never experienced any "Original" artist Lip-Sync. Note, I used the word Original! You see, the definition of Lip-Syncing is to move the lips silently in synchronization with a recorded soundtrack. What Freestyle artists are doing is not Lip-Syncing. They're simply performing along with, or over their own prerecorded vocals. In other words, there mics are live and loud. This is pretty standard among the genre, and in my opinion, quite okay. In fact, I encourage it, and I'll tell you why.

You see, during the initial recording, producers would have the artists overdub their vocals, a process that involved recording the same vocals several times across multiple tracks, layering it until it produced that big powerful sound that totally engulfs us. A song that features just one track of vocals will come across thin and dull, and every flaw will illuminate. Thousands of dollars in extended studio time has been invested into this part of the recording process because producers know that it makes the difference between a professional sounding product and one of an amateur. So if multiple vocal tracks are the key to that superior sound we've grown accustomed through continuous airplay, then why on earth would we even consider performing any other way? Look, the fans know who sang these songs, and there are enough music videos to confirm. So let's give the fans what they came for, a trip down memory lane, where they can sing along while reminiscing about a time when life was much simpler, instead of cringing each time you hit a note that wasn't supposed to be there in the first place.

The Process

I have been blessed with a very unique position in the

business, a position that has given me a better perspective of the Freestyle genre than most in my particular field. That position being from none other than the road! Whereas most booking agents are confined to the four walls of an office, I, for over twenty-five years have had the rare opportunity to experience the results of my very own deals first hand. From the actual performances of some of Freestyle's greatest artists of whom I've had the pleasure of booking, to the indescribable reactions of their fans, whether that be a good thing or not.

One of the questions I get asked all the time by new promoters, or at least those new to booking Freestyle is, what's the process? A very legitimate, not to mention smart question to ask, and that can only be answered by someone with experience. The process I will speak about here will be purposely simplified, with the hope that each time you run through it during your own events, that you modify it so that it is better and more efficient for you. The first part of the process that many do not take advantage of as much as they should is the Sound Check.

Sound Check

I'm going to try and detail this process as best as I can. Once I'm done you'll realize that it really isn't difficult, and if we're talking about Freestyle, the process doesn't change much from artist to artist. But knowing what to expect is going to put you at an advantage, and allow you to oversee the process, and be better prepared if anything were to go wrong. It all begins with the sound check. Freestyle shows are typically all track, and because of that, some people feel that a sound check isn't that important, but I'd have to disagree, because whenever you have an opportunity to make sure things don't screw up, I suggest you take it, and that's exactly what a sound check does, gives you that opportunity. When people speak of a Sound Check, the first thing they see is the word Sound, so of course that's the part that lingers, when in fact, the word that should linger more, should be the word *Check,* because that word is much more important. Yes, it's important to check the sound, make sure the mics work as well as the playback system, but here are some other things that should be "checked." Check from where the artist will be entering the club. Is there a private back door? Or do they have to come through the main entrance, because if so, then another Check comes into play. Security! Who are they? How many will there be and what post will be covered? Check out the club. The layout will make a whole lot more sense when it isn't dark and packed with hundreds of people. Check the VIP area, is it a place that seems comfortable and of course safe? Is this where the meet and greet session will take place? If so, is it set up properly, with a clear path for the fans to come in and out of without bumping into each other? Oh, and definitely check the stage itself, is it solid, and secure or wobbly with a bunch of holes in it? A problem for those artists who perform in heels.

So you get the idea, now let's take a quick look at the sound again. For a Freestyle track show we're technically dealing with usually three channels on the mixing board. Two channels for the music, and one for the microphone, and yeah, as the promoter, you wouldn't necessarily be the one dealing with this, but just think of the peace of mind you'd have knowing that if need be, you could step in at any point and run the show.

A great idea that would really put you ahead of the game is, get with your DJ, and have him teach you at least the basics. Start with hooking everything up. Nothing is going to give you a better idea about how a system works, than setting it up yourself. Learn it, and this would be one more part of the process that you'd feel more confident about. Another great reason to encourage sound checks, and at the very least, is to make sure that the system is compatible with the format from which the artist's store their music. You won't believe how many times I've seen acts discover minutes before they went on that the sound system didn't support their particular format, and what a mess that becomes! A sound check would've at least made them aware of the problem earlier, giving them time to correct it, whether that meant adding a piece of gear, or transferring the artist's track to a compatible format.

Fans pay to see these shows, and though Murphy has his own law, you as the promoter need to do everything possible to prepare for the inevitable, and with a plan B always on standby, you prove yourself to be not just a great promoter, but more importantly, a great problem solver!

Sound checks should be scheduled as early in the day as possible, reason being? It's usually a weekend when these shows are set, and if any equipment needs to be repaired or replaced, businesses would still be open. Figure out who will be handling your sound early on, and the sooner you can get that person in touch with the artist's road manager, the sooner they can start communicating in regards to the show, eliminating any possible surprises. Make sure before you bring the act to the venue for a sound check that everything is already connected and tested. The biggest waste of time is having acts stand around while the system is still being hooked up. Not only is it exhausting for the act, the pressure to hurry isn't a good thing to place on your tech team.

So, the act arrives at sound check and steps up on the stage. Pacing the stage he test its stability. The road manager hands the sound person the music to load and cue. The artist does a quick microphone check, and then signals the sound person that he's ready. It's during this time that the road manager should be "Sound Checking" the system. Can the artist comfortably hear through the stage monitors? Are there any hot spots that might cause feedback? Is the house system loud enough? The road manager should walk the room and make sure the sound is distributed evenly, keeping in mind that an empty room is going to have a much different sound than one packed with people, but either way, it should give him a pretty good idea of what to expect at show time.

If there's anything else that's needed, such as microphone stands, or props, now is the time to make sure they're available and working properly. If a lighting routine is a part of the show, then that needs to be sorted out and planned during sound check, because once the actual show begins, everyone's pretty much on their own!

Sound checks are NOT rehearsals. So an act running through their entire set makes absolutely no sense. If anything, they risk not only exhausting themselves, but also straining their vocals, and if there are other acts waiting to go next, then that's just being plain ol' rude and inconsiderate! They should only be checking a couple of minutes of sound, preferably from the beginning.

If the act has not collected the balance of their fee at

the hotel, then the sound check is where it should be settled. Having to deal with money moments before hitting the stage is never a good idea. Either the money is going to be miscounted, or the show schedule is going to be thrown off. Sometimes it's the promoter's policy to pay at the last minute, but if possible I try and suggest promoters pay earlier. Speaking of which, remember, deposits are usually fifty-percent, and sent to the booking agent upon signing. The balance however, is to be paid in cash the day of the show, and prior to the performance, and please, never rely on the door to cover the artist's balance, that money should always be available and on hand. Once the sound check has been completed, and all is well, confirm the pick-up time for the show so that everything stays on schedule, and if it's still early enough, why not invite the artist and his crew out to lunch, a perfect time to bond.

It's Show Time

Transportation should already be at the hotel by the time the artist gets to the lobby. Having an artist all dressed and ready to go, only to have them sit around the lobby waiting for their ride, can blast a serious hole in their adrenaline tank. The pick-up vehicle should come with only the driver. No friends, family or fans. This is a crucial time for the artist, and they need to get focused.

The driver should already know in which entrance the artist is to be brought in, this you went over at sound check. Security should be waiting, and the door unlocked. Two to four security guards, covering both the front and back of the artist, should get them backstage safely, and it's always a good idea to place them in a private area away from fans, preferably a dressing room, green room, or even an office can work. Autographs and photos before a show can be exhausting, so save that for afterwards. Make sure the artist and their crew has everything they need. Drinks, towels, water. Make them as comfortable as possible so that they can mentally prepare, stretch, yodel, or whatever it is they normally do before a show.

So, it's 11:30 PM and the show is about to begin. But wait! Who's going to introduce the performer? Well, if you ask me, I say you do it, the Promoter! That's right! When first starting out, *you* should be the one to Host the event. Don't try and be the DJ, serve drinks, bounce, or hang out with the artists. Host your own event! I mean, what better way to highlight yourself as the promoter than to put yourself up on that stage in front of your own audience and let them know who you are? Some promoters hire others to host their events, but why? I don't care who it is, people are not going to pack the house to see the host, and any host big enough *to* pack your place, isn't going to be interested in hosting it in the first place, so why not keep that opportunity for yourself? No one is going to be able to sell that artist better than you. No one is going to appreciate that audience as much as you, and no one is going to be able to set up that audience for the next event like you. So remember, host your own event!

So now that we've clarified that, I'll say it's a good idea that from the moment you lock in the act, that you begin working on your artist introduction, as well as other important things you might want to relate to your audience while you have their attention. So, you step up onto the stage and cue the DJ to lower the music. You spot the artist beside the stage, ready to go. You make eye contact with the road manager who should be by the sound system, and he gives you a thumbs up.

Greet your audience, thank them for coming, and then introduce the artist! It's always a good idea to get with the road manager to try and find out, what is an appropriate way to introduce them. I've heard host say some crazy things in the past, so don't ever assume they know, because whatever you relate to that audience, trust that they'll be taking it home with them that night.

Another important thing to keep in mind is, once you introduce the artist, get the hell off the stage! Don't stand there waiting for them to come to you. Know ahead of time if they want you to just place the mic on the stand and walk off, or hand it to them. These small details make for a smooth transition so they're very important, especially to the artist, besides, most of this should've already been situated during the what? That's right, The *Sound Check!*

Make sure the stage is clear. No one should be on it except the artist, unless the road manager specifies otherwise. Also, the stage should've already been checked, and if needed, cleaned of spilled drinks, cups, pocketbooks, phones etc.

While the artist is on stage, don't just stand there enjoying the show, study it! See what the act does, and how does the audience respond. Are people talking during the show? Going to the bathroom, or getting drinks? Does the audience seem bored, or fidgety? Or are they really into it? Take note, because in a year or so, it might be a good idea to bring that same act back.

So they make it to the end of their performance and everything was perfect, but watch carefully, because some acts like to address their audience after their performance, and you don't want to interrupt them, but once you see they're done, get the mic as they leave and head back on stage. The first thing you should tell your audience as you reach center stage is, "How about another round of applause, or something similar."

Make sure to announce any upcoming events, give a shout out to your staff, and plug your sponsors. Thank your audience for attending and then instruct your VIPs to start lining up for the meet and greet.

Meet and Greets

Yes, fans come to see their favorite acts perform their favorite Freestyle songs. But then they look forward to something else, and that being the highly anticipated Meet & Greet session. What is that? Well, just as the title says, it's a time allocated after the performance where the fans get to meet, and the artists get to greet. It's a special time for both sides and I always encourage it. Note, there are some acts that do not participate in Meet & Greets for whatever reason, so please make sure to check with your Booking agent and don't assume that Meet and Greets are a part of the show, because they're not. They're add-ons.

Artists have been blessed to be able to do what they do. They're blessed to have people want to not only see them perform, but to meet them. It is such a wonderful experience for the fans, and should be just as wonderful for the artists, so let's take a look at what it consist of, and realize that though it would be great if everyone at every event got the opportunity to meet the acts, that unfortunately, isn't always possible.

Meet & Greets have to be handled properly, because if

not, they can become a disaster, possibly even dangerous. Though I highly encourage them, I do not add them to my contracts. This is a service provided by the artist on a show to show basis, and relies totally on the safety, and comfortability of each particular artist. Comfortability is measured by the artist and staff from the moment they enter the club. Is there adequate security? Are they professional, and do they seem like they can control a problem? Are the fans behaving, or does it seem like they've already had too much to drink? And of course, having at least one local Police officer on staff for the night, gives everyone a little extra peace of mind. If the crowd isn't behaving, even if it's just one or two people, and nothings being done, there's a good chance the Meet and Greet will not happen. A venue that has continuous fights is a dangerous venue, and security shouldn't be there just to break fights up but more importantly to help prevent them from ever starting in the first place. Sounds like an impossible task? It's not! Ninety nine percent of the venues that we perform at have no fights. That's a huge percentage, reason being is these days, security has become really good at their jobs. They look the part, which makes patrons think twice about acting up.

So now onto the Meet & Greet. The first thing I look for, and this is usually done during sound check, is from where will the fans be entering and which way they will be exiting? If everyone is coming in and out of the same door, we're going to have a problem, so it needs to be moved. Again this is something that needs to be planned at sound check. Some places like to set up long tables for the acts to sit behind and sign autographs, and that's fine if autographs are all that's being offered. But nowadays smart phones keep cameras ready to point and shoot, so instead of trying to work against it, you need to try and work with it.

I've had the pleasure of being on the road with some of Freestyle's greatest female artists and I'll tell you, if you really want to learn how to road manage, road manage the women! The women of Freestyle are just like any other women, they love their shoes, and the higher the heel the more the love, and that's fine for a simple night on the town, but for a show, it comes with a whole bunch of challenges. Getting the women from the hotel to the car, the car to the club, to the dressing room which usually means walking through a kitchen whose already slippery floor is also covered with water and grease, which they end up taking with them to the wobbly stage whose seams are starting to separate, and thank God, because as of this writing, I have yet to have even one take a fall.

But then they get to the meet and greet, and though the smiles might say otherwise, rest assured, the feet are killing them, and having them stand for photos and then sit for autographs can be daunting, if not outright exhausting, and the quicker we exhaust the artist, the quicker that meet and greet will come to a halt. So here's a simple solution. Instead of the low table and chairs, place the artists behind a raised table, counter, or one of those round bar tables you find in practically every club. And give them stools so that they don't have to keep getting up and down between photos and autographs. I've been using this technique for quite a while now, and it works perfectly.

Let's play out a scenario so that you get a better idea of what I'm talking about. A couple step up to the artist, as the husband pulls out his phone. His wife strikes a pose beside the artist, and it's a Great shot! The two switch places but the wife, unfamiliar with hubby's phone, accidentally touches the wrong thing and the phone totally shuts down. The husband excuses himself and rushes over to his wife, resets the phone to camera, hands it back to her again and resumes position. Wife snaps the picture, but this time … there's no flash! Must I continue?

This situation is way too common. It happens at just about every event, and with a hundred plus people on line and only an hour for the meet and greet, chances of us getting to everyone doesn't seem too promising. So, how do we handle this? Well, first off, while the fans are still on line, make sure they have their phones set to camera and flash ready to go. No one should be searching through their pocketbooks for their phones while the artists sit there waiting. Another approach would be for you to appoint someone from your staff to assist with these photos. As each person enters the VIP area, the assistant would take their phone, which should be set and ready to go, and takes the photo. If it's a couple we can get both people in the picture with the artists, having now expedited the entire process by fifty percent. This works like a charm, and believe it or not, the fans understand and appreciate the effort you'll be making to get everyone in. Oh, and please, just one snap each, they don't need three different angles.

Now let's talk about security for a minute as I cannot stress enough, its importance. First off, if you are supplying the security yourself, what you want more than 3rd degree black belts, are guys who are intimidating enough to keep problems at their absolute minimum. I know I'm repeating myself here, but it's important. You don't need to hire people to break up fights. You need people to help prevent them from ever happening in the first place.

One security person should be posted at the entrance of the VIP area. His job would be to control the incoming traffic, while keeping an eye on the artist and be ready to move if something were to go wrong inside the VIP.

The moment the autograph is signed and the photo is taken, security posted beside the artist should quickly direct the traffic toward the VIP exit, where another security guy stands to let them out.

Another idea I came up with years ago, and have seen work like a charm, is to hire a professional photographer, or at least someone with a good camera and maybe some lighting. Have that photographer take all the photos, and post them the next day onto your website, or Social Media page, allowing fans to go in and take what they want. Don't charge them for this service. Make it free, as a sort of thank you to those who attended. This is a great marketing tactic as well because it sends people to your page where of course you'll be advertising your next Freestyle event. Another great investment that you can make is in a backdrop that you can place behind the artists during photos. This is a great way of not only marketing your brand, but also your sponsor's. It'll also work as a reminder to the fans as to where and when they got to take that picture with their favorite Freestyle artist.

So, your club holds a thousand people, does that mean the artist has to sign a thousand autographs? Not at all! Many promoters make the Meet & Greet available only to their VIP ticket buyers. These tickets will cost a bit more than the general admission, so they'll have to be limited. Make sure to consult with your booking agent about this, as the last thing you want to do is start promoting something that isn't likely to happen.

SIMPLE STEP #7

LET'S DO IT AGAIN

James Rios: Once the show is over and everything and everyone has been taken care of, I go home shower and go to bed. Good or bad, there is nothing I can do about it now. The next morning I wake up and personally take the artist to the airport and then I evaluate the show and try to figure out what I could've done better, and did I represent myself and my company the right way? After about a week, I start to think about what I should do next. Never plan more than one show at a time.

So, you did it! You put on your first event and everything went smooth, and now you can honestly call yourself a Freestyle Club Promoter. That's right. And please, use the word Freestyle, don't be ashamed. Don't just call yourself a Promoter, call yourself a *Freestyle* Promoter! This is the genre that launched your career, so hold it high. Now tell me, was it fun? Did you make money? What did you learn? Like most businesses, it might take a few go-rounds before you truly get the hang of it. But I can pretty much guarantee you this, especially dealing with this genre, if you keep it going, you're only going to get better. If you take each situation, whether it was good or bad and learn from it, then every event will be a little more successful than the last.

Chuck Lamagra: *Always be planning your next event. I make sure we have announcements ready, and if possible, even flyers to give out. Word of mouth and viral marketing always starts the night of the previous show. The one time that I didn't do this, I noticed my ticket sales dropped by about 15%.*

You should never approach another event with the same mentality as you had with the last. There should be a new focus. Your plan should not be the same, and each time your bar should be set just a bit higher. Know what worked, and what didn't, and figure out why. Make the bad stuff good, and the good stuff better. Figure out what areas you feel you spent too much money, and where you feel you should've invested more.

Just because you don't have an event coming up, doesn't mean that you shouldn't stay in touch with your audience. Find a reason to stay connected. Do not allow yourself to leave their minds. Instead of once a month, ask the club owner if you can promote something every week, doesn't have to have an artist, could be just a DJ. And if you're not making anything on those nights, that's fine, consider it as an investment in the big picture, and another way of staying in touch with your audience.

JI Starr: *Make sure that everyone involved gets paid! If you don't, you will never develop a loyal crew. Always plan your next event way ahead of time. Have a short celebration if you made money, or at least broke even.*

Freestyle events are all pretty much the same, regardless of who's throwing them. So try your best to be different, and don't be afraid of taking it outside the box. The acts are all going to be the same, they're going to sing the same songs, and their routines are not going to change much from show to show, so for the sake of the fans, *you* make the change! Think of different themes you can implement into your event, different hooks that would make you stand out among the others. This is how you as a promoter can really show off your talents and skills. This is what will breathe new life into our genre, and inspire it to grow and expand.

I'll say it again, Social Media is a Godsend to anyone in any business, you just have to figure out how to make it work for you, but once you do, it is going to be a powerful tool. As of this writing Social Media is full of pages and groups dedicated to Freestyle Music. The platforms are there, the fans are there, all you have to do now if figure out how to get them to your particular event. If you rely simply on the line-up, your event is going to share just about the same success as every other. There probably isn't a Freestyle artist left that has yet to be seen by the masses, but think about it, if nothing changes then why would the fans want to keep paying to see the same thing over and over again? The answer is, most of them won't, which means only one thing... Poor ticket sales!

Nick Huminski: Every event has a life of its own. There are 100 moving parts to each event. Once the event ends the machine stops. take time to reflect on the event and work to improve on the things that you could do better next time.

You can't go to the artists and ask them to change their show, instead you need to change the platform from which that show is presented. Amusement parks for example, all have Roller Coasters, but there are only so many twists and turns one can come up with, so what makes people flock to one roller coaster as opposed to another? Usually the theme! And how it works is they take the same loops and dips, and rearrange them a bit differently. They then add lights and exciting colors, backgrounds, music, and of course a cool name, because if it isn't cool, then the kids won't ride it. The same idea can be applied to Freestyle events, and if done right, you can create for yourself the opportunity to book outside the regulars. You can give other artists a shot without worrying too much about their individual drawing power. How great would this be for the genre as a whole? Freestyle is much bigger than most realize, and today new material is still being recorded. If we were to compile all of the Freestyle music that's been recorded over the last thirty years, I bet we would have one of the largest music catalog's in existence.

Here is something else that is very important, in fact any new promoter that I come in contact with, I usually tell them this; Consistency will be the key to your success, which is why in any business, the Marathon makes more sense than the twenty yard dash. Pace yourself and focus on the long haul because that is the true course. As I've mentioned, Freestyle events are probably the most affordable music genres to promote, but you need to plan for consistency, and longevity. If you run too fast at the beginning, you're going to tire quickly. So set your sights, take a deep breath, and just enjoy the trip.

Charlie Rodriguez: I never have time to celebrate. While one show is on, the next one is already being promoted. In fact, I use my in-house facility to promote the next show. You are only as good as your last show. What you did today is gone, turn the page and keep going.

I myself as an agent have always tried to help keep my promoters in business by helping them plan out there events at least a year in advance. Doesn't mean we have to sign up that far out, or even put down any money, but to at least have an idea of the direction and caliber of the artist you want to bring in will put you way ahead of the game.

One very important thing that I've not only told every promoter I've worked with, I've also seen them want to kick themselves for not listening to me, and believe me when I tell you, if you don't listen now, you'll want to kick yourself as well. Once you open up a market to Freestyle events, as long as you stay consistent with a quality event happening at least once a month, you will indeed own that territory. But don't for once think that you aren't being watched. Oh but you are! And the moment you turn your back on that market, just once, believe me when I tell you, someone else will quickly hop in that bed, and if they're smart and have been watching your moves, they'll know how to pick up right from where you left off.

Luis Pinto: After a show I usually say, Never Again! But something always tends to pull me back in, usually when I'm approached by someone about investing.

So in conclusion to this topic, my advice would be to have your second event already sketched out before you even begin your first. Don't sketch in pen, sketch in pencil because as you build your first event, you're going to learn a few things, and you need to be able to adjust your sketch accordingly. If you want to maintain the consistency of an event once a month, you cannot wait till you are done with the first to begin the second, they practically have to go hand in hand, not to mention that first event would be the perfect time to promote your second, so you need to be able to take full advantage of that. Remember, you cannot announce artist appearances without first having them locked in, meaning with a contract and deposit, because there is no guarantee that they'll even be available for the date. And to get everyone excited about an event, just to have to go and change it on them, will surely throw a wrench into the business you are trying to build.

Hassan Martinez: I'm promoting my next show, while saying goodbye, goodnight and thanks for coming out.

FINAL WORDS

I reached out to about fifteen potential Mentors before deciding on these seven, and I think I made a wise choice. If you'd like to get in touch with any of them, they're all available through Social Media, or you can reach out to me and I will be more than happy to help you connect. So with that said, I want to thank each of these promoters for their gracious contributions to the The 7 Simple Steps, and wish them a lifetime of success and happiness. But, before I let them go, I wanted to ask each of them if they had any final words or advice for the readers, and this is what they said:

Charlie Rodriguez: *Being a promoter is not something you aspire to do when growing up. You do not attend college and receive a degree in promotions. You have to love what you do, if you do not have a passion for it, don't even mess with it. This journey began as a tribute to my brother, Sal who passed away. His favorite artist was "Stevie B." I was a Police Officer at the time, so I put a show together titled Cop-Aid, and couldn't believe it when over 10,000 people showed up. Freestyle and Disco music touches a lot of people, and is the soundtrack to many of their lives. I myself love it so much, that I now have my own radio station called Miami One. Look, I once lost $75,000 In one night, but if you are passionate enough, not even that will stop you.*

Luis Pinto: *Save toward not needing investors.*

James Rios: *The first thing you must understand is being a promoter is not for everyone, and you should really decide if this is something you have the stomach for. You will win some and lose some, but it's the loses that will make you a better promoter. We all learn from our mistakes, and some of those mistakes can be quite costly. If a promoter tells you he or she has never lost, they are lying, so run away from those clowns. Remember it's a business and you can't take it personal. You made the choice to do it, so never blame anyone else. I truly believe that the secret to all success is what I refer to as, K.I.S.S.(Keep It Simple Stupid)*

Chuck Lamagra: *There is money to be made, things to learn, and fun stuff to get involved with, but you won't know this unless you get in there and give it a try.*

Nick Huminski: *In most cases you'll only have one chance, so use your energy wisely. Don't get distracted by what everyone else is doing. Stay focused and only concentrate on your own event. Don't follow the Yellow Brick Road... Create it!*

Hassan Martinez: *Stay humble...*

JI Starr: *Never let the risk stop you from at least trying. As long as you have a burning desire to succeed, there will be no problem you can't overcome. Partner with established promoters or club owners and learn what you need to know in order to break out on your own. Good Luck to you, and remember, its not impossible!*

CLOSING

So there you have it, folks. Seven simple steps to get you on your way, to a successful career with Freestyle Club Promotions. And before you get there, because I know you will, let me be the first to congratulate you, and also thank you. I will be here for all of you. I will try and answer any questions I could and help you in any way possible, with absolutely no strings attached. Remember,

if you know the process, have the right people in place, you can do it. And as much as I would love to see you hit a home run from the start, be prepared for a few base hits at first. But as long as you don't give up, you will eventually make it to home plate.

The keys to a successful promoting career, are the same keys for the success of any business. Persistence, consistence, and knowledge. If you really want to make this happen, you have to be persistent. You have to push forward with all you have. There has to be no excuses as to why you can't do it. Whether that means seeking funds, a venue, a team, a particular artist or whatever. Put whatever it is that you need at the forefront of your mind, visualize and create a step by step plan on how to obtain that. It's like whipping up a steak dinner, complete with a baked potato and a side of steamed vegetables, and desert. You can't just whip it all up at once, you have to do it in steps, because some things take a little bit longer to prepare than others. But the more you do it, the easier it becomes, and the better it taste, until finally, no one can make a steak dinner as fast, or as good as you!

Don't let time be the problem. If it is, write down your day and keep track of it. What time do you wake up? What time do you go to sleep? And then, what are you doing through each hour in between? I can guarantee you that there is enough time being wasted for you to replace it with an activity that will help improve on your promotional skills.

Next! Be consistent! In other words, don't stop! Work on your craft every single day. Over and over again, until you get it right, and once you get it right, work on it some more to make it even better. Mike Tyson, the former heavy weight champion of the world, wasn't born a champ. He was born just like the rest of us, except he discovered his passion early in life. That passion is what makes it easy to be disciplined, and discipline is what we need to develop our craft, which will eventually make us the champs we were meant to be.

Then there's knowledge. Every time you put on an event, the most valuable thing that you can take from it, even more than the money it makes, is the experience! You see, money you spend, and it's gone. But experience you get to keep and recycle over and over again! How amazing is that?

And don't ever think you know it all, because you don't, and until you are honest with yourself about that, you will not seek that knowledge and that will eventually place your career into stagnicity.

I want to thank you all for picking up a copy of The 7 Simple Steps. And as you take on this new venture, or build your existing venture to the next level, and suddenly you hear someone sort of whisper in your ear, saying to get up, and push because you can do it. That will be me. Cheering you on.

I pray that Freestyle music gives to you, the gifts that it has given to me. Thank you. Thank you all so much, and please, find me on Social Media, and let's be friends!

- Latif Mercado

ABOUT THE AUTHOR

Road managing Lil' Suzy had given Latif Mercado opportunities he could never have imagined, like when he was promoted to Exclusive Booking Agent after another was caught redirecting her inquires. This move helped get Suzy onto the promoter's most requested list, and by expanding his artist roster to include other big names, Latif's company, La' Entertainment, became the Go-to Agency, for Freestyle Club and Concert Events everywhere!

In this first of its kind book entitled, Freestyle Promotions, and the 7 Simple Steps to Getting Started, the author, with the help of some friends, shares his twenty plus years of experience, and unique perspective as a Booking Agent, in hopes of inspiring a new generation to try their hand at this very exciting, and lucrative career. Latif believes that the promoters are indeed the lifeline of the Freestyle Music genre, and has his own vested interest in their success.

#LatifMercado is active on Social Media, and loves hearing and interacting with his readers.

GLOSSARY

All-In (All Inclusive) a fee paid to cover a service and all of its necessary expenses to enable digital
storage and transmission.

Back line - audio amplification equipment for bands, set up behind the stage, such as amplifiers for
guitars or synthesizers.

Bar Guarantee - a certain amount of bar sales that you guarantee a club or venue will generate on the night of your event, and if failed to meet the sales specified in the guarantee, you as the club promoter would pay the difference.

Brand - a product or service developed by a person or company under a particular name.

Booking Agent - someone who engages a person or company for performances.

Contract - a document that defines the legal relationship between a promoter and an artists.

Deposit - a sum payable as a first installment on the purchase of something or as a pledge for a contract,
the balance being payable later.

Expenses - cost of extras outside of Artist Fee which may include, flights, hotel, ground transportation,
riders, food, etc.

Freestyle Music - a form of electronic dance music created by the Urban Latino youth of New York City in the 1980s,

Freestyle Phony - a person intentionally deceiving a promoter or audience into believing that they are a particular Freestyle Artist in order to charge a fee for their performance.

Genre - a category of artistic composition, as in music or literature, characterized by similarities in form, style, or subject matter.

Interest - money paid regularly at a particular rate for the use of money lent, or for delaying the repayment of a debt.

Investor - a person or organization that puts money into financial schemes, property, etc. with the expectation of achieving a profit.

Lip-Sync - to move ones lips Silently in synchronization with a recorded soundtrack.

Meet and Greet - an organized event during which a celebrity, politician, or other well-known figure gets to meet and greet the public.

MP3 - a means of compressing a sound sequence into a very small file.

Nightclub - an establishment for nighttime entertainment, typically serving drinks and offering music, dancing, etc.

Original - of origin. Not fake or phony.

Promoter - individuals or companies responsible for organizing a live **concert** tour or special event performances.

Rider (Performance Rider) - A set of request or demands that a performer sets as criteria for
performance. Types of riders include hospitality and technical.

ROI (Return On Investment) - expressed as a percentage and is typically used for personal financial decisions, to compare a company's profitability.

Remix - a new or different version of a recorded song that is made by changing or adding to the original
recording.

Road Manager - a part of the management team that physically accompanies the artists while on the road. Road Manger responsibilities include organizing travel, confirming accommodations, conducting sound checks, collecting balances, and assuring the safety of their artists.

Social Media - computer-mediated technologies that facilitate the creation and sharing of information, ideas, career interests and other forms of expression via virtual communities and networks.

Sound Check - the preparation that takes place before a concert, or similar performance, where the sound crew runs through a small portion of the upcoming show to make it's producing clear sound at the right volume and balance.

Sponsor - a person or organization that provides funds for a project or activity carried out by another, in particular.

Stagnicity - the state of being stagnant. Showing no activity; dull and sluggish.

Track show - when a performer sings along with a prerecorded track of music.

NOTES:

I'd Like To
Hear From You

@LatifMercado

www.ingramcontent.com/pod-product-compliance
Lightning Source LLC
Chambersburg PA
CBHW071002040426
42443CB00007B/621